Welfare

Other Books in the Issues on Trial Series:

Welfare

Sylvia Engdahl, Book Editor

GREENHAVEN PRESS
A part of Gale, Cengage Learning

GALE
CENGAGE Learning

Detroit • New York • San Francisco • New Haven, Conn • Waterville, Maine • London

Christine Nasso, *Publisher*
Elizabeth Des Chenes, *Managing Editor*

© 2011 Greenhaven Press, a part of Gale, Cengage Learning

For more information, contact:
Greenhaven Press
27500 Drake Rd.
Farmington Hills, MI 48331-3535
Or you can visit our Internet site at gale.cengage.com.

For product information and technology assistance, contact us at

Gale Customer Support, 1-800-877-4253
For permission to use material from this text or product, submit all requests online at www.cengage.com/permissions

Further permissions questions can be emailed to permissionrequest@cengage.com

Articles in Greenhaven Press anthologies are often edited for length to meet page requirements. In addition, original titles of these works are changed to clearly present the main thesis and to explicitly indicate the author's opinion. Every effort is made to ensure that Greenhaven Press accurately reflects the original intent of the authors. Every effort has been made to trace the owners of copyrighted material.

Cover Image © Jim West/Alamy.

LIBRARY OF CONGRESS CATALOGING-IN-PUBLICATION DATA

Welfare / Sylvia Engdahl, book editor.
    p. cm. -- (Issues on trial)
  Includes bibliographical references and index.
  ISBN 978-0-7377-5110-9 (hardcover)
  1. Public welfare--Law and legislation--United States--Juvenile literature. 2. Welfare recipients--Legal status, laws, etc.--United States--Juvenile literature. I. Engdahl, Sylvia.
    KF3720.W45 2011
    344.7303'16--dc22

                                                                    2010030744

Printed in the United States of America
1 2 3 4 5 6 7 14 13 12 11 10

Contents

Until the late 1960s investigators in many states spied on single mothers to find out if they had male partners in their homes. Besides being an invasion of privacy, these policies prevented such women from forming relationships that might lead to marriage or at least to financial help from a partner. Activists demonstrated against the policy and eventually filed lawsuits challenging it.

Chapter 2: Welfare Payments Cannot Be Terminated Without a Hearing

Chapter 3: Eligibility for Welfare Can Be Conditioned on Consent to Home Visits

A law professor argues that the precedent set by *Wyman v. James* has made it nearly impossible to challenge the constitutionality of home visits to welfare recipients on Fourth Amendment grounds, as is shown by the opinion in *Sanchez v. County of San Diego*, a case in which the visits were being made by district attorney fraud investigators rather than social workers.

Chapter 4: Welfare Recipients Who Move to Another State Are Entitled to Its Benefits

Foreword

The U.S. courts have long served as a battleground for the most highly charged and contentious issues of the time. Divisive matters are often brought into the legal system by activists who feel strongly for their cause and demand an official resolution. Indeed, subjects that give rise to intense emotions or involve closely held religious or moral beliefs lay at the heart of the most polemical court rulings in history. One such case was *Brown v. Board of Education* (1954), which ended racial segregation in schools. Prior to *Brown*, the courts had held that blacks could be forced to use separate facilities as long as these facilities were equal to that of whites.

For years many groups had opposed segregation based on religious, moral, and legal grounds. Educators produced heartfelt testimony that segregated schooling greatly disadvantaged black children. They noted that in comparison to whites, blacks received a substandard education in deplorable conditions. Religious leaders such as Martin Luther King Jr. preached that the harsh treatment of blacks was immoral and unjust. Many involved in civil rights law, such as Thurgood Marshall, called for equal protection of all people under the law, as their study of the Constitution had indicated that segregation was illegal and un-American. Whatever their motivation for ending the practice, and despite the threats they received from segregationists, these ardent activists remained unwavering in their cause.

Those fighting against the integration of schools were mainly white southerners who did not believe that whites and blacks should intermingle. Blacks were subordinate to whites, they maintained, and society had to resist any attempt to break down strict color lines. Some white southerners charged that segregated schooling was *not* hindering blacks' education. For example, Virginia attorney general J. Lindsay Almond asserted, "With the help and the sympathy and the love and re-spect of the white people of the South, the colored man has risen under that educational process to a place of eminence and respect throughout the nation. It has served him well." So when the Supreme Court ruled against the segregationists in *Brown*, the South responded with vociferous cries of protest. Even government leaders criticized the decision. The governor of Arkansas, Orval Faubus, stated that he would not "be a party to any attempt to force acceptance of change to which the people are so overwhelmingly opposed." Indeed, resistance to integration was so great that when black students arrived at the formerly all-white Central High School in Arkansas, fed-eral troops had to be dispatched to quell a threatening mob of protesters.

Nevertheless, the *Brown* decision was enforced and the South integrated its schools. In this instance, the Court, while not settling the issue to everyone's satisfaction, functioned as an instrument of progress by forcing a major social change. Historian David Halberstam observes that the *Brown* ruling "deprived segregationist practices of their moral legitimacy. . . . It was therefore perhaps the single most important moment of the decade, the moment that separated the old order from the new and helped create the tumultuous era just arriving." Considered one of the most important victories for civil rights, *Brown* paved the way for challenges to racial segregation in many areas, including on public buses and in restaurants.

In examining *Brown*, it becomes apparent that the courts play an influential role—and face an arduous challenge—in shaping the debate over emotionally charged social issues. Judges must balance competing interests, keeping in mind the high stakes and intense emotions on both sides. As exempli-fied by *Brown*, judicial decisions often upset the status quo and initiate significant changes in society. Greenhaven Press's Issues on Trial series captures the controversy surrounding in-fluential court rulings and explores the social ramifications of such decisions from varying perspectives. Each anthology highlights one social issue—such as the death penalty, students' rights, or wartime civil liberties. Each volume then focuses on key historical and contemporary court cases that helped mold the issue as we know it today. The books include a compendium of primary sources—court rulings, dissents, and immediate reactions to the rulings—as well as secondary sources from experts in the field, people involved in the cases, legal analysts, and other commentators opining on the implications and legacy of the chosen cases. An annotated table of contents, an in-depth introduction, and prefaces that overview each case all provide context as readers delve into the topic at hand. To help students fully probe the subject, each volume contains book and periodical bibliographies, a comprehensive index, and a list of organizations to contact. With these features, the Issues on Trial series offers a well-rounded perspective on the courts' role in framing society's thorniest, most impassioned debates.

Introduction

Poverty has always been among the most serious problems facing society, and since the beginning of the twentieth century it has been one of the most controversial. Before then, it was an accepted fact of life that a segment of the population—in most eras a large segment—would remain too poor to afford basic necessities. During the past hundred years many people have begun to hope that poverty can someday be eliminated. Whether or not it can, most people now feel that aid to the poor is an essential aspect of civilization.

In early America some poor people were supported by charity, while those not so fortunate lived as beggars or indentured servants. In the nineteenth century, state governments became involved. An 1824 New York law specified that paupers applying for relief must be sent to the county poorhouse, and if they refused to do the work assigned there or tried to escape, they should be placed in solitary confinement and fed only bread and water. This law also stated that "it shall and may be lawful for the overseers of the poor of any town or city in said county, to take up any child under the age of fifteen years, who shall be permitted to beg or solicit charity from door to door, or in any street or highway of such city or town, and carry or send him or her to said poor-house, there to be kept and employed, and instructed in such useful labor as he or she shall be able to perform."

The poorhouse system arose from the common belief that poor people were morally inferior to those who could support themselves and were undeserving of more than an absolute minimum of assistance. Later, state laws were modified, especially with regard to veterans of the Civil War and, by 1875, children, who were exempted from poorhouse confinement. Nonetheless, the poor were still looked down upon. Poverty was felt to be their own fault, except in the case of "worthy" individuals such as widows. Not until the twentieth century did this attitude slowly begin to change, accelerated by provision of aid to World War I veterans and victims of the Great Depression of the early 1930s, during which many formerly employed people lost their jobs.

The Depression led to the New Deal, legislation passed during President Franklin D. Roosevelt's administration. These laws gave the federal government much more power over citizens' lives than it had previously held. One of these laws was the Social Security Act of 1935, which instituted the first welfare system, Aid to Dependent Children (ADC; later named AFDC for Aid to Families with Dependent Children). Although ADC was a federal program, it was administered by the states, and the states decided who received its benefits. Because most of the poor were still widely regarded as "undeserving," many states set their eligibility criteria in such a way as to exclude people whose lifestyles met with disapproval. During the 1960s activists opposed these limits, and in 1968 the first legal challenge to them that reached the Supreme Court, *King v. Smith*, established that aid to poor children was a benefit to which they were entitled under the law—a concept subsequently known as entitlement. Children could not be denied aid on grounds that their mother's lifestyle was immoral in the eyes of the state.

The ADC/AFDC program had problems from the beginning. It did not provide enough money to lift families out of poverty, and yet the outcome most feared by its opponents— that some people would cheat and collect benefits to which they were not entitled, or would choose to remain on welfare instead of trying to get work—did come to pass in some cases. Furthermore, the program created a large government bureaucracy that was costly and involved red tape that hindered receipt of aid by the truly needy. By the 1990s the majority of Americans wanted welfare reform, and under a law passed in 1996, AFDC was replaced by a somewhat different program called Temporary Assistance to Needy Families (TANF). Aid through TANF is not an entitlement; there are strict requirements that must be met before a person can collect benefits, and there is a time limit on how long he or she can receive them. Its primary goal is to reduce the number of people on welfare by getting them into jobs, or training them for jobs if they are not already qualified.

TANF has indeed cut the welfare rolls; the number of recipients dropped from over 14 million in 1994 to 5.8 million by 2000. The significance of this is controversial. Have more than half the former recipients become less poor, or is there now more unmet need? Have most mothers once on welfare gotten work that supports them, or are they worse off than before, either because their jobs pay too little or because they were disqualified for technical reasons despite being unable to find jobs? There are sharp differences of opinion as to whether the program has been a success.

These differences reflect a fundamental division in public attitudes toward welfare and welfare recipients. Some people believe that it is the government's responsibility to provide for the needs of the poor and for it not to do so is unjust and inhumane. Others believe that the public should not be forced to support the poor—because after all, government money comes from taxpayers, not only the rich but those whose own income is not large—and that far from helping poor people, giving them money routinely rather than merely on an emergency basis harms them by preventing them from gaining self-sufficiency. Opponents of government welfare programs believe private charities can help the needy more effectively.

A further complication is that there is even more disagreement than in the past about whether the government should use financial means to further majority views of morality. In the past, it was generally believed that having babies out of wedlock was an unqualified sin. Today, many Americans still believe this and are convinced that the best way to reduce poverty is to discourage single parenthood; a major goal of TANF is to eliminate illegitimacy, promote marriage, and foster traditional family values. But others believe that lifestyle is a matter of personal choice and that women who want babies should not be penalized for having them, whether they are married or not. They feel that the idea that all children should be supported by fathers is obsolete now that women's roles in society have changed, and that pushing mothers into unwanted relationships with men, some of whom might turn out to be abusive, benefits neither the women nor their children.

One aspect of morality on which Americans do agree is that people should not cheat the government and that welfare fraud should be prevented. Unfortunately, in any society some people do cheat. There are people who try to collect welfare despite having income that they conceal, for example; or they claim to have children that do not actually exist. So the question arises, how much burden should be placed on the majority of welfare recipients, who are honest, in the attempt to catch those who are not? The detection of fraud requires investigation, and investigation inevitably involves invasion of privacy. Where is the line to be drawn? Is it a violation of constitutional rights to investigate all recipients in order to keep limited funds from being diverted to cheaters? This is an issue that has sometimes come before the courts.

Conflicting opinions about the role of the government in reducing poverty are based on a deeper conflict between differing political philosophies, and can therefore never be wholly resolved. The nation's welfare policy has changed over time and will continue to change. The aim must be to find the best possible balance between opposing views.

Denying Welfare Payments Based on an Unmarried Mother's Morality

Case Overview

King v. Smith (1968)

King v. Smith was the first welfare case ever heard by the Supreme Court. It arose from welfare rights activists' efforts to end discrimination against poor people who behaved in ways considered immoral, discrimination that until the 1960s had been accepted by the public as natural and desirable. Whether there was also racial discrimination involved in these policies is controversial; more blacks were affected than whites, but analysts have pointed out that poverty was more prevalent among blacks.

One of the policies most objectionable to welfare recipients and their supporters was known as the "substitute father" or "man-in-the-house" rule, under which Aid to Families with Dependent Children (AFDC) benefits (commonly known as "welfare") were denied to single mothers who had had or were having sexual relationships with men they were not married to. Women on welfare were allowed no privacy with regard to their personal lives; caseworkers made surprise visits to their homes to see whether a man was present and sometimes even spied on them elsewhere. This was viewed as a reasonable way of reducing the number of welfare recipients; when funds were insufficient to provide adequately for all poor families, it was felt that the money available should go to the most "deserving"—those who adhered to society's moral standards. Policy makers also wanted to reduce illegitimate births, although a 1960 federal regulation prohibited direct denial of assistance to children on grounds of their illegitimacy.

States attempted to justify the "substitute father" rule by assuming that a man living in a home, or frequently visiting, served as a father to the children there and probably contributed money to their support. In that era, it was taken for granted that families were supported by men, except in the case of a widow who had no men in her life. For this reason, married couples were not eligible for welfare benefits; the husband was expected—and in fact legally required—to provide for the kids. Supporters of the "substitute father" rule argued that it was not fair for unmarried couples to receive benefits when married ones did not, although in reality a single woman's boyfriend was not obliged to support her children and seldom did so.

Sylvester Smith, a poor black woman with four children, lived in a shack on the outskirts of Selma, Alabama. She earned $20 a week as a waitress. From time to time she was visited by a married man named Willie Williams, who went home in the morning to his wife and nine children. In 1966 Smith wrote a letter to President Lyndon Johnson complaining that her welfare payments were inadequate, which was forwarded to Alabama welfare officials. Shortly thereafter, her caseworker, who had become suspicious that Smith had a live-in boyfriend, wrote to tell her that her welfare benefits were being cut off under Alabama's "substitute father" law. Lawyers with the Center on Social Welfare Policy and Law, who wanted to challenge such laws and were on the lookout for suitable plaintiffs for a test case, heard about Smith and decided that among several they were considering, her situation gave them the best chance of winning. Their strategy was to claim that the law discriminated against African Americans.

The district court ruled in Smith's favor, finding that the substitute father regulation violated the equal protection clause of the Fourteenth Amendment to the Constitution by denying benefits to needy children on a basis not related to their need for aid; however, the court did not agree that it was a racial discrimination case. "This decision should be and will be designed to enure to the benefit of all needy children regardless of their race or color," the court said. "The Equal Protection

Clause is not restricted in its application to the protection of the rights of Negroes. It is more far-reaching, protecting the rights of any identifiable class."

The state of Alabama appealed to the U.S. Supreme Court, whose decision was unanimous. It ruled that the substitute father regulation violated the federal Social Security Act, under which children who are legally fatherless cannot be denied aid on grounds of what the Court called the "transparent fiction" that they have a substitute father. There is indeed a rational reason for differentiating between married and unmarried couples' eligibility for aid, it said, because a man not married to the children's mother has no legal obligation to support them.

The Supreme Court's ruling affected about five hundred thousand children nationwide, and it was also hailed as a victory for welfare recipients' right to privacy. Mothers could still be investigated, however, on the chance that they really were receiving unreported income. Furthermore, it did not eliminate interference with poor women's personal choice of lifestyle, for it specifically upheld the states' rights to deal with "conduct it regards as immoral" and to remove children from "unsuitable" homes, as long as the children were not deprived of the financial aid to which the AFDC program entitled them.

> *"It is simply inconceivable ... that Alabama is free to discourage immorality and illegitimacy by the device of absolute disqualification of needy children."*

Majority Opinion: Fatherless Children Are Entitled to Support Regardless of Their Mother's Relationships

Earl Warren

Earl Warren was the chief justice of the United States from 1953 to 1969. Prior to that he was governor of California and the Republican nominee for vice president in the 1948 presidential election. Warren was one of the most influential Supreme Court justices in U.S. history, but he was also among the most controversial, as many of his decisions conflicted with traditional views. In the following opinion from King v. Smith, *he rules that states may not deny welfare benefits to mothers on the grounds that the mothers have relationships with men who are not their husbands. Alabama's general power to deal with the problems of illegitimacy and behaviors it regards as immoral is not in question, he says, but it is not permissible for the state to exercise that power in a way detrimental to needy children. In the Court's opinion the claim that it is unfair to give welfare payments to unmarried mothers when married ones are ineligible is not valid, because a woman's husband is legally required to support*

Earl Warren, majority opinion, *King v. Smith*, U.S. Supreme Court, June 17, 1968.

her children whereas other men with whom she is involved are not. Calling such a man a "substitute father" does not absolve the state of its obligation to provide assistance to needy children, wrote Warren.

The AFDC [Aid to Families with Dependent Children; that is, welfare] program is one of three major categorical public assistance programs established by the Social Security Act of 1935. The category singled out for welfare assistance by AFDC is the 'dependent child,' who is defined in § 406 of the Act, as an age-qualified 'needy child who has been deprived of parental support or care by reason of the death, continued absence from the home or physical or mental incapacity of a parent, and who is living with' any one of several listed relatives. Under this provision, and, insofar as relevant here, aid can be granted only if 'a parent' of the needy child is continually absent from the home. Alabama considers a man who qualifies as a 'substitute father' under its regulation to be a nonabsent parent within the federal statute. The State therefore denies aid to an otherwise eligible needy child on the basis that his substitute parent is not absent from the home.

Under the Alabama regulation, an 'able-bodied man, married or single, is considered a substitute father of all the children of the applicant mother' in three different situations: (1) if 'he lives in the home with the child's natural or adoptive mother for the purpose of cohabitation'; or (2) if 'he visits (the home) frequently for the purpose of cohabiting with the child's natural or adoptive mother'; or (3) if 'he does not frequent the home but cohabits with the child's natural or adoptive mother elsewhere.' Whether the substitute father is actually the father of the children is irrelevant. It is also irrelevant whether he is legally obligated to support the children, and whether he does in fact contribute to their support. What is determinative is simply whether he 'cohabits' with the mother.

The testimony . . . by officials responsible for the administration of Alabama's AFDC program establishes that 'cohabitation,' as used in the regulation, means essentially that the man and woman have 'frequent' or 'continuing' sexual relations. With regard to how frequent or continual these relations must be, the testimony is conflicting. One state official testified that the regulation applied only if the parties had sex at least once a week; another thought once every three months would suffice; and still another believed once every six months sufficient. The regulation itself provides that pregnancy or a baby under six months of age is prima facie evidence of a substitute father.

Between June 1964, when Alabama's substitute father regulation became effective, and January 1967, the total number of AFDC recipients in the State declined by about 20,000 persons, and the number of children recipients by about 16,000 or 22%. As applied in this case, the regulation has caused the termination of all AFDC payments to the appellees, Mrs. Sylvester Smith and her four minor children.

Mrs. Smith and her four children, ages 14, 12, 11, and 9, reside in Dallas County, Alabama. For several years prior to October 1, 1966, they had received aid under the AFDC program. By notice dated October 11, 1966, they were removed from the list of persons eligible to receive such aid. This action was taken by the Dallas County welfare authorities pursuant to the substitute father regulation, on the ground that a Mr. Williams came to her home on weekends and had sexual relations with her.

Three of Mrs. Smith's children have not received parental support or care from a father since their natural father's death in 1955. The fourth child's father left home in 1963, and the child has not received the support or care of his father since then. All the children live in the home of their mother, and except for the substitute father regulation are eligible for aid. The family is not receiving any other type of public assistance, and has been living, since the termination of AFDC payments, on Mrs. Smith's salary of between $16 and $20 per week which she earns working from 3:30 a.m. to 12 noon as a cook and waitress.

Mr. Williams, the alleged 'substitute father' of Mrs. Smith's children, has nine children of his own and lives with his wife and family, all of whom are dependent upon him for support. Mr. Williams is not the father of any of Mrs. Smith's children. He is not legally obligated, under Alabama law, to support any of Mrs. Smith's children. Further, he is not willing or able to support the Smith children, and does not in fact support them. . . .

States Must Furnish Aid

Provisions of the Act clearly require participating States to furnish aid to families with children who have a parent absent from the home, if such families are in other respects eligible.

The State argues that its substitute father regulation simply defines who is a nonabsent 'parent'. . . . The State submits that the regulation is a legitimate way of allocating its limited resources available for AFDC assistance, in that it reduces the caseload of its social workers and provides increased benefits to those still eligible for assistance. Two state interests are asserted in support of the allocation of AFDC assistance achieved by the regulation: first, it discourages illicit sexual relationships and illegitimate births; second, it puts families in which there is an informal 'marital' relationship on a par with those in which there is an ordinary marital relationship, because families of the latter sort are not eligible for AFDC assistance.

We think it well to note at the outset what is not involved in this case. There is no question that States have considerable latitude in allocating their AFDC resources, since each State is free to set its own standard of need and to determine the level of benefits by the amount of funds it devotes to the program. Further, there is no question that regular and actual contributions to a needy child, including contributions from the kind of person Alabama calls a substitute father, can be taken into account in determining whether the child is needy. In other words, if by reason of such a man's contribution, the child is not in financial need, the child would be ineligible for AFDC assistance without regard to the substitute father rule. The appellees here, however, meet Alabama's need requirements; their alleged substitute father makes no contribution to their support; and they have been denied assistance solely on the basis of the substitute father regulation. Further, the regulation itself is unrelated to need, because the actual financial situation of the family is irrelevant in determining the existence of a substitute father.

Also not involved in this case is the question of Alabama's general power to deal with conduct it regards as immoral and with the problem of illegitimacy. This appeal raises only the question whether the State may deal with these problems in the manner that it has here—by flatly denying AFDC assistance to otherwise eligible dependent children.

Changing Attitudes Toward Welfare

Alabama's argument based on its interests in discouraging immorality and illegitimacy would have been quite relevant at one time in the history of the AFDC program. However, subsequent developments clearly establish that these state interests are not presently legitimate justifications for AFDC disqualification. Insofar as this or any similar regulation is based on the State's asserted interest in discouraging illicit sexual behavior and illegitimacy, it plainly conflicts with federal law and policy.

A significant characteristic of public welfare programs during the last half of the 19th century in this country was their preference for the 'worthy' poor. Some poor persons were thought worthy of public assistance, and others were thought unworthy because of their supposed incapacity for 'moral regeneration.' This worthy-person concept character-ized the mothers' pension welfare programs, which were the precursors of AFDC. Benefits under the mothers' pension pro-grams, accordingly, were customarily restricted to windows who were considered morally fit.

In this social context it is not surprising that both the House and Senate Committee Reports on the Social Security Act of 1935 indicate that States participating in AFDC were free to impose eligibility requirements relating to the 'moral character' of applicants. During the following years, many state AFDC plans included provisions making ineligible for assistance dependent children not living in 'suitable homes.' As applied, these suitable home provisions frequently disqualified children on the basis of the alleged immoral behavior of their mothers.

In the 1940's, suitable home provisions came under in-creasing attack. Critics argued, for example, that such dis-qualification provisions undermined a mother's confidence and authority, thereby promoting continued dependency; that they forced destitute mothers into increased immorality as a means of earning money; that they were habitually used to disguise systematic racial discrimination; and that they sense-lessly punished impoverished children on the basis of their mothers' behavior, while inconsistently permitting them to re-main in the allegedly unsuitable homes. In 1945, the predeces-sor of HEW [Department of Health, Education, and Welfare] produced a state letter arguing against suitable home provi-sions and recommending their abolition. Although 15 States abolished their provisions during the following decade, nu-merous other States retained them.

In the 1950's, matters became further complicated by pres-sures in numerous States to disqualify illegitimate children from AFDC assistance. Attempts were made in at least 18 States to enact laws excluding children on the basis of their own or their siblings' birth status. All but three attempts failed to pass the state legislatures, and two of the three successful bills were vetoed by the governors of the States involved. In 1960, the federal agency strongly disapproved of illegitimacy disqualifications.

Nonetheless, in 1960, Louisiana enacted legislation requiring, as a condition precedent for AFDC eligibility, that the home of a dependent child be 'suitable,' and specifying that any home in which an illegitimate child had been born subsequent to the receipt of public assistance would be considered unsuitable. In the summer of 1960, approximately 23,000 children were dropped from Louisiana's AFDC rolls. In disapproving this legislation, then Secretary of Health, Education, and Welfare [Arthur S.] Flemming issued what is now known as the Flemming Ruling, stating that as of July 1, 1961,

> A State plan may not impose an eligibility condition that would deny assistance with respect to a needy child on the basis that the home conditions in which the child lives are unsuitable, while the child continues to reside in the home. Assistance will therefore be continued during the time efforts are being made either to improve the home conditions or to make arrangements for the child elsewhere.

The Flemming Ruling

Congress quickly approved the Flemming Ruling, while extending until September 1, 1962, the time for state compliance. At the same time, Congress acted to implement the ruling by providing, on a temporary basis, that dependent children could receive AFDC assistance if they were placed in foster homes after a court determination that their former homes were, as the Senate Report stated, 'unsuitable because of the immoral or negligent behavior of the parent.'

In 1962, Congress made permanent the provision for AFDC assistance to children placed in foster homes and extended such coverage to include children placed in child-care institutions. At the same time, Congress modified the Flemming Ruling by amending § 404(b) of the Act. As amended, the statute permits States to disqualify from AFDC aid children who live in unsuitable homes, provided they are granted other 'adequate care and assistance.'

Thus, under the 1961 and 1962 amendments to the Social Security Act, the States are permitted to remove a child from a home that is judicially determined to be so unsuitable as to 'be contrary to the welfare of such child.' The States are also permitted to terminate AFDC assistance to a child living in an unsuitable home, if they provide other adequate care and assistance for the child under a general welfare program. The statutory approval of the Flemming Ruling, however, precludes the States from otherwise denying AFDC assistance to dependent children on the basis of their mothers' alleged immorality or to discourage illegitimate births.

The most recent congressional amendments to the Social Security Act further corroborate that federal public welfare policy now rests on a basis considerably more sophisticated and enlightened than the 'worthy-person' concept of earlier times. State plans are now required to provide for a rehabilitative program of improving and correcting unsuitable homes, to provide voluntary family planning services for the purpose of reducing illegitimate births, and to provide a program for establishing the paternity of illegitimate children and securing support for them.

In sum, Congress has determined that immorality and illegitimacy should be dealt with through rehabilitative measures rather than measures that punish dependent children, and that protection of such children is the paramount goal of AFDC. In light of the Flemming Ruling and the 1961, 1962, and 1968 amendments to the Social Security Act, it is simply inconceivable, as HEW has recognized, that Alabama is free to discourage immorality and illegitimacy by the device of absolute disqualification of needy children. Alabama may deal with these problems by several different methods under the Social Security Act. But the method it has chosen plainly conflicts with the Act.

Alabama's Second Justification

Alabama's second justification for its substitute father regulation is that 'there is a public interest in a State not undertaking the payment of these funds to families who because of their living arrangements would be in the same situation as if the parents were married, except for the marriage.' In other words, the State argues that since in Alabama the needy children of married couples are not eligible for AFDC aid so long as their father is in the home, it is only fair that children of a mother who cohabits with a man not her husband and not their father be treated similarly. The difficulty with this argument is that it fails to take account of the circumstance that children of fathers living in the home are in a very different position from children of mothers who cohabit with men not their fathers: the child's father has a legal duty to support him, while the unrelated substitute father, at least in Alabama, does not. We believe Congress intended the term 'parent', to include only those persons with a legal duty of support.

The Social Security Act of 1935 was part of a broad legislative program to counteract the Depression. Congress was deeply concerned with the dire straits in which all needy children in the Nation then found themselves. . . . The AFDC program, however, was not designed to aid all needy children. The plight of most children was caused simply by the unemployment of their fathers. With respect to these children, Congress planned that 'the work relief program and the revival of private industry' would provide employment for their fathers. . . .

The AFDC program was designed to meet a need unmet by programs providing employment for breadwinners. It was designed to protect what the House Report characterized as '([o])ne clearly distinguishable group of children.' This group was composed of children in families without a 'breadwinner,' 'wage earner,' or 'father,' as the repeated use of these terms throughout the Report of the President's Committee, Committee Hearings and Reports and the floor debates makes perfectly clear. To describe the sort of breadwinner that it had in mind, Congress employed the word 'parent.' A child would be eligible for assistance if his parent was deceased, incapacitated or continually absent.

The question for decision here is whether Congress could have intended that a man was to be regarded as a child's parent so as to deprive the child of AFDC eligibility despite the circumstances: (1) that the man did not in fact support the child; and (2) that he was not legally obligated to support the child. The State correctly observes that the fact that the man in question does not actually support the child cannot be determinative, because a natural father at home may fail actually to support his child but his presence will still render the child ineligible for assistance. On the question whether the man must be legally obligated to provide support before he can be regarded as the child's parent, the State has no such cogent answer. We think the answer is quite clear: Congress must have meant by the term 'parent' an individual who owed to the child a state-imposed legal duty of support. . . .

We think it beyond reason to believe that Congress would have considered that providing employment for the paramour of a deserted mother would benefit the mother's children whom he was not obligated to support.

By a parity of reasoning, we think that Congress must have intended that the children in such a situation remain eligible for AFDC assistance notwithstanding their mother's impropriety. . . .

A contrary view would require us to assume that Congress, at the same time that it intended to provide programs for the economic security and protection of all children, also intended arbitrarily to leave one class of destitute children entirely without meaningful protection. Children who are told, as Alabama has told these appellees, to look for their food to a man who is not in the least obliged to support them are without meaningful protection. Such an interpretation of congressional intent would be most unreasonable, and we decline to adopt it. . . .

The pattern of this legislation could not be clearer. Every effort is to be made to locate and secure support payments from persons legally obligated to support a deserted child. The underlying policy and consistency in statutory interpretation dictate that the 'parent' referred to in these statutory provisions is the same parent as that in § 406(a). The provisions seek to secure parental support in lieu of AFDC support for dependent children. Such parental support can be secured only where the parent is under a state-imposed legal duty to support the child. Children with alleged substitute parents who owe them no duty of support are entirely unprotected by these provisions. . . . If Alabama believes it necessary that it be able to disqualify a child on the basis of a man who is not under such a duty of support, its arguments should be addressed to Congress and not this Court.

State Objectives Not Defected

We think it well, in concluding, to emphasize that no legitimate interest of the State of Alabama is defected by the decision we announce today. The State's interest in discouraging illicit sexual behavior and illegitimacy may be protected by other means, subject to constitutional limitations, including state participation in AFDC rehabilitative programs. Its interest in economically allocating its limited AFDC resources may be protected by its undisputed power to set the level of benefits and the standard of need, and by its taking into account in determining whether a child is needy all actual and regular contributions to his support.

All responsible governmental agencies in the Nation today recognize the enormity and pervasiveness of social ills caused by poverty. The causes of and cures for poverty are currently the subject of much debate. We hold today only that Congress has made at least this one determination: that destitute children who are legally fatherless cannot be flatly denied federally funded assistance on the transparent fiction that they have a substitute father.

> "A needy mother of any race whose aid
> is denied because she is married would
> be right in asking why her neighbor
> who lives with a man out of wedlock
> should get a welfare check."

Appellants' Brief: Denying Welfare Payments on the Basis of a Woman's Relationships Is Reasonable

MacDonald Gallion et al.

MacDonald Gallion was the Alabama attorney general during King v. Smith. *In the following brief replying to the brief filed by the lawyers for Sylvester Smith in* King v. Smith, *he argues that Alabama's policy of denying welfare benefits to women who have relationships with men to whom they are not married is a reasonable means of allocating funds. He asserts that if the state did not deny benefits to such people, a greater number of needy people would experience hardship because the state's lack of money would force reductions in benefits to all current recipients. There is no evidence of racial discrimination in the application of this policy, he says. In his opinion there is nothing wrong with discouraging people from living together out of wedlock. Moreover, since married couples are not eligible for welfare, they would consider it unfair for unmarried ones to receive it.*

In Alabama an otherwise needy dependent child is ineligible for public assistance if there are two able-bodied parents in the home. In a situation where parents are legally married, the

MacDonald Gallion et al., appellants' brief, *King v. Smith*, U.S. Supreme Court, April 18, 1968.

father may not (1) give economic support or (2) give love and affection; in a situation where a husband is the stepfather of the children he may not owe a legal duty of support to the children; yet in all of these situations the children are not eligible for AFDC [Aid to Families with Dependent Children] and this conforms with state and federal requirements. Obviously this requirement exists because it is believed that the taxpayer, and the state and federal governments representing the taxpayer, do not wish to encourage dependency, unemployment, or any effort to escape work on the part of parents by permitting them to rely on a regular monthly grant for the child from the government rather than seeking to support them by working. Undoubtedly there are instances of hardship in situations where persons are married to each other, and it is clear that the Alabama public assistance categories only purport to help those persons who fit within these regulations which carve out those general groups of persons the State elects to assist within the framework of the Social Security Act and applicable federal regulations. "Needy" in every State in the Union is always subject to particular definitions at particular times depending upon available federal money, state money and the laws or regulations developed by Congress, HEW [Department of Health, Education, and Welfare], the State legislature or State Welfare Boards defining the "most needy." . . .

The substitute parent regulation was not plucked out of the air in an arbitrary, whimsical manner. As we have shown, it was a reasonable means which the Department of Pensions and Security selected to narrow the class eligible for AFDC benefits and thus avoid the hardship which would have been caused to a far greater number of recipients by a reduction of the maximum amount of benefits allowable. The mere fact that some different classification *could*, or even as Appellees contend *should* have been made, is not a matter which addresses itself to the courts. . . .

Racial Discrimination Not Established

Appellees [represented by Sylvester Smith] have altogether failed to establish that there has been racial discrimination in the formulation or application of the regulation. . . . We do not believe that Appellees have shown that they are being subjected to an unfair regulation which is being applied in a discriminatory fashion. . . .

The facts in this case show that the percentage of the AFDC caseload as it relates to members of the Negro race steadily increased during the time the regulation was in effect and there is no evidence that the Alabama Negro population has increased proportionally. Appellees have cited no drastic employment crises or other reasons why the caseload would have risen to offset this obvious fact. There is no evidence that any white person has been treated differently.

When viewed in the light of the resources the state has to strengthen family life and rehabilitate AFDC families, it does not seem invidious to say *no* to persons living together out of wedlock if aid is also denied when there are two able-bodied married parents. In a state with limited resources it is most important that the public assistance recipients themselves feel a sense of fairness. A needy mother of any race whose aid is denied because she is married would be right in asking why her neighbor who lives with a man out of wedlock should get a welfare check.

The regulation does affect many members of the Negro race. To fail to say *no* to practices which do not help the low income groups achieve economic wholeness does not honor the very low income groups nor the Negro families who have come from slavery to responsible citizenship and leadership. Abraham Lincoln observed that you cannot help men permanently by doing for them what they could and should do for themselves. At this moment in our history is a paternalistic differentiation required? Does a firm "No" dishonor any low income member of any race? The Social Security Act has as one of its objectives the goal of stopping dependency upon the government. That the Alabama regulation approaches the problem from the standpoint of the negative is not unlike the Bill of Rights, which to preserve the dignity of individual man, tells government what it cannot do. . . .

The Alabama agency does want a rule which will best help the mother to say "no" to situations which do not help her or which result in more children who need care at government expense. The Alabama agency does not have the complete answer to that question, but early returns from the study that is now being made of the caseload affected, which is available since the vacation of Justice [Hugo] Black's original stay Order, shows some very positive results of the regulation.

Promiscuity Helps No One

Although, as pointed out by one of the *amici* [friends of the court] briefs, the Alabama regulation does not require complete chastity as a condition precedent to public aid in Alabama, it does seem to require that the mother agree to some degree of continence. Is there anything really *bad* about continence? Does the literature of the New Morality or the Kinsey Reports [on human sexual behavior] actually prove that continence is not a better way of life? Unbridled sex in this country recently has been more stylish. But a number of practices in the American society have been "stylish" before this court reversed the trends. Can it really be seriously advanced that informal living arrangements and unruly promiscuity actually help the poor or the affluent? The lower Court said "The approval or disapproval of sexual promiscuity is not here involved;" maybe welfare agencies will believe this, and maybe learned lawyers who know how to group and regroup legal theories will believe this—maybe many very well meaning organizations who want very much to help the low income members of society have more than they now have will believe this—but will the low income married family who does not receive a public assistance check and who sees the post-man deliver one to the neighbor in similar economic circumstances who does live out of wedlock believe this? . . .

Without being moralistic, hypocritical or puritanical, there is much to be said for continence. It would be a most refreshing breeze to blow over this country. Imagine turning on television and listening to programs which not only extolled continence and chastity but which also pointed out the attractive aspects of purity. Appellants submit that the important reason that married low income families and the public wants the AFDC mother to be able to say "no" is really because there is a great longing in everyone for all mothers, poor and affluent, to say "no." There is no government grant or service which would give more to an AFDC child—or any other child—than a social order which, again, makes it wholesome and stylish for a mother to say *No* to adultery and fornication.

Nature places a great privilege and a great responsibility on women. Neither Appellees nor *amici* have shown exactly why saying a judicial *yes* to cohabitors out of wedlock is going to help a deserted mother, widow, or unwed poor mother or affluent mother get a husband—particularly one who is apt to be helpful with the children. It may be an extremely old fashioned notion, but Appellants advance that the opposite is more nearly true (not that merely getting a husband would necessarily solve all of her problems).

In the long run continence and chastity make better homes. Continence and chastity make better mothers and fathers. This is true for affluent fathers and mothers and poor fathers and mothers. The Alabama agency does not think this Court would apply such a public policy matter differently to an affluent family in an analogous situation. The mere fact that the question coming to this Court affects poor persons right now does not mean that this Court would later set up another rule of law for the affluent.

There appears to be a belief held among many that sexual relations are necessary to health. This belief could have been the motive for Appellee Smith's statements that she intended to maintain a relationship with some man. Appellants deny the validity of this belief and assert that chastity does accord with good health.

Alabama Regulation Strengthens Family Life

This court in viewing questions on rights of privacy and self-incrimination can refuse to be led off on all sorts of tangents which could make it difficult for States to make such classifications, and by looking very closely at the confidentiality statutes can recognize that these statutes do protect the AFDC mother. This Court can also recognize that this regulation relates to future conduct and like *Gardner* [*v. State of Alabama Department of Pensions*] does *not* condemn past conduct. The regulation says to the mother "Go and 'cohabit out of wedlock' no more" just like *Gardner* says to persons who supply services to the poor "Go and discriminate, because of race no more" if you want the public assistance payment. . . .

Appellants submit that the AFDC mother who brought this suit has been benefitted by the regulation. Appellants submit that in Alabama the regulation comes closer to achieving the purposes of the Social Security Act—to "strengthen family life" than an opposite course of action in view of the fact that the regulation operates in a State where aid is denied "able-bodied" families when there is a marriage. Obviously the adultery and fornication statutes are not effective vehicles for meeting the Twentieth Century's public interest in strengthening family life. Recognizing that a welfare agency is not apt to achieve total continence on the part of the poor (or anyone else) and with full knowledge that the agency would not be in this Court if it knew all of the answers to informal practices and with full recognition that getting checks and services to needy families is the primary responsibility in the AFDC program, Appellants do urge this Court to grant whatever relief is meet [fit] and proper in the premises.

"The substitute parent rule not only prohibited women's contact with the fathers of their children, but also encouraged invasions of their privacy."

Women Were Subject to Invasion of Privacy by Welfare Investigators

Anne M. Valk

Anne M. Valk is a professor of history and associate director of programs for the John Nicholas Brown Center at Brown University. In the following viewpoint she explains the substitute-father rule under which, prior to the Supreme Court's decision in King v. Smith, *some states denied welfare benefits to women who had relationships with men to whom they were not married. She describes the means used to enforce it, such as surprise night visits to homes, and she explains the tactics used by activists in the attempt to end these practices. Welfare recipients hailed the Court's ruling as a victory in their struggle for privacy, she says, but officials, fearing that the increase in the number of families eligible for welfare benefits would exceed available funds, continued their efforts to uncover fraud.*

Women ... battled to control their sexual behavior by challenging the restrictive substitute parent rule. Along with pressuring welfare recipients to use contraception, this rule gave welfare authorities a means to limit the number of children added to welfare rolls. In the District [of Columbia]

Anne M. Valk, "Mother Power: The Movement for Welfare Rights in Washington, D.C., 1966–1972," *Journal of Women's History*, vol. 11, no. 4, 2000, pp. 42–44. Copyright © 2000 The Johns Hopkins University Press. Reproduced by permission.

and eighteen states, the man-in-the-house or substitute parent regulation denied public funds to dependent children in families where a second adult, presumed to be a male partner, potentially contributed support. The regulation disqualified aid to a child whose mother was determined to be in a sexual relationship, regardless of whether the man had any legal responsibility to the family. The presumption of responsibility, along with the means used to determine cohabitation, deterred women from forming relationships. The substitute parent rule not only prohibited women's contact with the fathers of their children, but also encouraged invasions of their privacy. Looking for male partners residing in a household, D.C. investigators conducted surprise night searches of homes. They interviewed friends, neighbors, relatives, and ministers; snooped in bank accounts; talked to moneylenders; and scanned insurance company records for any evidence of unreported income. Local welfare workers viewed the man-in-the-house rule as a necessary means to discourage welfare "cheats" and channel public monies only to the deserving. Members of the Senate Subcommittee on District of Columbia Appropriations, a central component of the welfare department's operations, regularly budgeted funds to increase the investigative staff; between October 1961 and November 1967, the number of investigators hired to identify fraudulent claims grew from five to seventy-seven employees.

In contrast, welfare activists consistently pressured the welfare department to end this practice. They considered the man-in-the-house provision as a way to punish women who attempted to form two-parent households and as closing off a possible exit from poverty. Because the women perceived that the welfare department exercised so much authority, they likened it to "a jealous husband" who required women to "justify their existence to caseworkers, friends, family, and 'public opinion,'" [writes Nancy Young in *Off Our Backs*, November 1971]. Some women had terminated marriages for similar behavior and thus resented such constrictions from the city agency. Because welfare caseworkers determined families' eligibility to receive AFDC [Aid to Families with Dependent Children] funds, the women felt powerless individually to challenge or disregard the regulation. Indeed, at least one woman who refused to admit welfare inspectors into her home was subsequently denied public assistance, an incident that no doubt reinforced fear of the repercussions of acting alone. By essentially prohibiting relationships with men, the requirement consigned women and their families to managing on a single income, an amount typically inadequate whether it came only from public assistance funds or from public money combined with income from a low paying job.

Activists Fought to Overturn Rule

Welfare activists employed a variety of approaches to publicize their opposition to investigations and overturn the policy. They regularly held demonstrations to highlight the issue, including staging a "lie-in" which blocked the parking lot of the District's welfare department offices, and picketing the house of a welfare department administrator. In 1966, Neighborhood Legal Services lawyers filed a class action suit on behalf of AFDC recipients against the city's board of commissioners and local welfare department officials. *Smith v. Board of Commissioners* attacked the man-in-the-house rule. The welfare recipients and their lawyers lost the case in fall 1966, but a suit against Alabama's man-in-the-house rule toppled the regulation. In June 1968, the Supreme Court ruled in *King v. Smith* that the Alabama law violated federal welfare policy, thus invalidating similar statutes across the country. The Court's ruling, however, left welfare departments with a justification to continue home inspections: *King v. Smith* invalidated the denial of AFDC funds in cases where a man held no legal ties to a family. But welfare departments could deny AFDC funds in cases where an able-bodied natural or adoptive father was legally responsible to support his children.

Still, Washington's AFDC recipients hailed the Court's decision as a victory in their struggle for privacy and stability in their family lives by increasing their chances to marry and move off welfare rolls. In contrast, welfare officials worried that in light of the decision the number of families eligible for public assistance would further exceed funds. Between 1966 and 1972, the number of families receiving AFDC steadily grew, the result of NWRO's [National Welfare Rights Organization] successes in broadening eligibility requirements and publicizing available benefits. Even before the Court's ruling, the District's welfare department failed to convince Congress to increase its budget. Given its financial restrictions, the department announced that despite the Court's ruling it would still review cases to "get facts on financial resources, family composition, and living arrangements." But, in 1969, the D.C. City Council responded to welfare activists' pressure and moved to discontinue unannounced investigations. Congressional appropriations committees, assuming that the dramatic growth in D.C.'s welfare rolls stemmed from fraudulent eligibility claims, still pushed for home inspections to minimize expansion of welfare cases. Even though they claimed insufficient resources to increase public assistance grants to recipients, federal and local officials funneled more money into investigations to uncover fraud.

> "King is ... troubling insofar as it tac-
> itly accepts the argument that moral
> intervention in the intimate lives of
> poor families constitutes a legitimate
> governmental activity."

King v. Smith Endorsed Government Efforts to Promote Morality

Anna Marie Smith

*Anna Marie Smith is a professor in the Department of Govern-
ment at Cornell University. She won the American Political Sci-
ence Association's Victoria Schuck Award in 2008 for the best
book on women and politics for* Welfare Reform and Sexual
Regulation, *from which the following excerpt is taken. In it, she
describes the background of* King v. Smith *and argues that although the Supreme Court ruled that welfare benefits could not
be denied to a mother because she had a relationship with a
man to whom she was not married, it nevertheless endorsed the
idea that the government should promote morality. The Court
approved government measures to remove children from homes
it deemed unsuitable and to encourage birth control. Furthermore, Smith asserts, the Court implied that in accepting welfare
benefits, poor women give up their right to be left alone and to
make their own decisions about sexuality.*

Anna Marie Smith, *Welfare Reform and Sexual Regulation.* New York: Cambridge University Press, 2007. Copyright © Anna Marie Smith 2007. Reprinted with the permission
of Cambridge University Press.

We can put child support enforcement into its historical context by examining the 1968 *King* decision. As one of its many protest strategies, the welfare rights movement challenged the constitutionality of AFDC law in the courts. Under the Assistance to Dependent Children program (ADC, which was later named Assistance to Families with Dependent Children, or AFDC), the states revived the demanding moral requirements that had been central to the mothers' pensions, such that they were able to restrict eligibility and to protect their local labor markets from upward pressures on the wage scale. In addition, the ADC/AFDC program became a vehicle through which the state and federal governments could showcase their specific ideas about family values. Like the reformers who designed the mothers' pension schemes, FDR's [President Franklin D. Roosevelt's] policy experts in the 1930s took for granted the universal desirability of the family wage model. In an ideal household, children were reared by a legally married heterosexual couple. The father/husband would earn the family income while the mother/wife would bear and rear the children and look after her husband's personal needs. In an iteration of the Madonna/whore distinction, official and popular discourse divided needy mothers into two categories, the deserving widow and the loose woman. This distinction was given much more prominence in 1939 when widows and their children were shepherded into the survivors' insurance program. As the states set up their own ADC programs, they adopted the "substitute father" rule as one of the most potent tactics for restricting program eligibility.

Under the AFDC program rules of several states—especially the states in the South—any adult male who was present in the home could be considered a "substitute father" who was avoiding his natural duty to support his needy family. Investigative procedures—which sometimes included nighttime raids and police surveillance—were widely adopted to monitor the number of adults living in the same residence.

Some states adopted an "unsuitable home" rule; like the "substitute father" rule, it served as an effective tool for arbitrary denials of applications and expulsions on moral grounds. In one particularly outrageous case, AFDC caseworkers went undercover in their town's outdoor "lovers' lanes" to look for recipients who were allegedly carrying on extra-marital affairs. A few states went so far as to prohibit AFDC coverage for poor children if their biological parents were not "ceremonially married." They even brought criminal prosecutions under fornication laws against the poor women who bore children out of wedlock. Because AFDC assistance often constituted the only form of public support that a poor mother could obtain, the strict and arbitrary eligibility rules also meant that she had to think twice before leaving an abusive partner. In this sense, the AFDC program contributed not only to the regulation of the low-wage labor market, but to the policing of the poor single mother's intimate life as well.

AFDC Policies Racially Biased

African American women particularly singled out for the worst types of AFDC's sexual policing. The "substitute father" rule, the "unsuitable home" rule, and the ban on out-of-wedlock children were systematically used in such a racially biased manner that they virtually became a proxy for racial exclusion. The AFDC programs operated by the southern states were particularly harsh; they routinely subjected African American women to the most aggressive forms of moral policing. In addition, they determined that some women were "employable mothers." Unlike the other women in the program, the "employable mothers" were expected to take work in the fields and in domestic service whenever it was available. Black women and Latinas were especially targeted where these work requirements were concerned.

The *King* case originated as a constitutional challenge to Alabama's "substitute father" rule mounted by poverty rights advocates. The state's AFDC program excluded families from receiving benefits where it found that the mother was "cohabiting" with a man outside of marriage. Officials for the state testified that "cohabitation" existed wherever the man and woman in question had "frequent" or "continuing" extramarital sexual relations. The Court noted that various officials offered conflicting definitions of the minimum level of frequency of sexual relations necessary to establish sufficiently disqualifying "cohabitation," ranging from once a week to once every six months. The state's AFDC regulations further stipulated that a pregnancy or a baby under six months of age constituted prima facie evidence of a "substitute father." Alabama's use of the term "substitute father" is revealing. From the perspective of the state authorities, the poor single mother's secret male partner was giving cash under the table to the mother and her children, and those funds were not being properly declared to the welfare agency as family income. It was bad enough that public funds were going to single-mother-headed families, but the idea that the state had to subsidize extramarital sex among loose women and their production of an endless stream of bastard children was insupportable. (It was widely believed by medical and political elites that women of color and poor women lacked the intelligence necessary to use contraceptives.) The sexual relationship between the poor single mother and the "substitute father" was taking place out of wedlock. If her parents would not do the right thing by driving the male lover to the church altar with a shotgun, then the state was going to step in to do the next best thing. It would cut off the family's benefits.

Did Not Rule Out Government Intervention

In *King*, the Court responded to the constitutional challenge mounted against the "substitute father" rule in a complex manner. . . . The Court struck down the "substitute father" rule on the grounds that it violated the statutory entitlement of needy American families. It stated that as long as the Social Security Act defined the purpose of the AFDC program in the following terms—"aid to families with dependent children shall be furnished with reasonable promptness to all eligible individuals"—then the states could not use the "substitute father" rule to keep needy families off the rolls. . . .

[But] *King* is . . . troubling insofar as it tacitly accepts the argument that moral intervention in the intimate lives of poor families constitutes a legitimate governmental activity. The Court found that the only problem with Alabama's "substitute father" was that it disqualified needy children from receiving benefits. Across-the-board exclusion would not be allowed, but disciplinary forms of inclusion were perfectly reasonable. Parroting the very language used by the authorities that had wielded such arbitrary powers over the poor for decades—if not for centuries—the Court said that the State was perfectly welcome to take "rehabilitative" measures to "improve and correct" "unsuitable" homes among AFDC recipients. It cited, with approval, the efforts that the federal government had recently made to remove needy children from homes deemed "unsuitable" on moral grounds. This intervention was perfectly acceptable to the Court as long as those children continued to receive poverty assistance when they were placed in the foster care system. It did not matter that the states were not actually demonstrating that the mothers in question had "abused" their children in an objective sense and in proper legal proceedings; the governmental interest in the rearing of children within "morally suitable" homes trumped the parental rights of these poor women. . . .

Further, the Court applauded a particular type of State-sponsored "family planning" in *King*, citing, with evident approval, government programs designed to encourage the use of birth control among women who are needy, who already have children, and who are considered to be predisposed toward bearing children outside of marriage. Once the governmental interest is framed in this manner, it seems perfectly legitimate for the State to embrace a racially skewed and moralistic approach to poverty policy. Considered from this perspective, it makes no sense to propose macroeconomic reforms that would address the inegalitarian distribution of income and the structural impediments to equal opportunity in the capitalist marker; what is needed is the moral correction of the wayward poor single mother.

There is a logical connection, then, between the three policy invitations that the Court issues in *King*—namely, child support initiatives, family planning for poor women, and the intensification of child removal on the basis of neglect. Once official discourse accepts the idea that the family wage and the patriarchal, marital, and heterosexual family are the preferred social institutions for protecting the household from poverty, then it seems perfectly legitimate for officials to decide that impoverishment among families headed by single women is caused by these women's immoral behavior and father/husband absence. The poor mother does not need a caregiver's entitlement, protection from racial and sexist discrimination, subsidized childcare, access to high-quality further education, or—should she decide to combine caregiving with wage earning—a well-paying job located in a family-friendly workplace. She has to get married, or she has to stop having children and give up her children for adoption. Further, the Court gives its endorsement to the idea that the poor tacitly surrender their right to be left alone when they turn to the State for assistance. It is hard to imagine, for example, the Supreme Court inviting the states to promote "family planning" for America's middle class in the late 1960s. The dependence of the poor upon the public purse makes them uniquely appropriate candidates for State interventions that would otherwise be abhorrent.

In other words, *King* strikes down the "substitute father" rule and yet at the same time upholds much of the obnoxious thinking that lies behind the rule. The Court's recognition of the statutory entitlement to poverty assistance in *King* arguably constitutes one of its most egalitarian and democratic moments. But because the *King* Court also signals that it will allow the federal and state governments to promote heterosexual marriage, child removal, race- and class-targeted birth control, and marriage-like arrangements such as mandatory child support for poor families in the context of the AFDC program, it puts its seal of approval upon the policing of poor women's sexuality.

> "Federal policies that were instituted during [the 1960s] . . . continue to contribute to our national woes."

King v. Smith Caused the Child Poverty Rate to Climb

Janice Shaw Crouse

Janice Shaw Crouse is a former speechwriter for President George H.W. Bush and is a political commentator for the Concerned Women for America Legislative Action Committee. In the following viewpoint she argues that the Flemming Rule, which established that eligibility for welfare cannot be denied on grounds that a woman's children are illegitimate, and the Supreme Court decision in King v. Smith, *which ruled that welfare cannot be denied because the mother has a relationship with a man not her husband, have been harmful to the nation. She says that since these rulings, far more children are living in poverty than before, there are ten times as many unmarried couples living together, and the number of female-headed households with children has increased by 250 percent. In her opinion these developments were caused by these government actions and have negative ramifications because, among other reasons, the poverty rate of children in mother-only households is five times higher than in married-couple families.*

Suddenly, there is great interest in the 1960s. Senator Barack Obama explained in a Fox News interview that Senator Hillary Clinton couldn't bring the country together because she was still fighting the battles of the 60s. [The November 19,

Janice Shaw Crouse, "Beverly LaHaye Institute: 1968 Policies and Election 2008," *Concerned Women for America*, November 26, 2007. Reproduced by permission.

2007,] *Newsweek* cover story features the year 1968 as the year that made us who we are. [Emeritus news anchor] Tom Brokaw has a book coming out about the voices of the 60s. Obviously, the "Boomers" aren't going to leave the scene quietly.

Lots of folks have lots to say about the people and the events of the "Age of Aquarius"—the student occupation of administration buildings on campuses across the nation, the violent demonstrations against the war in Vietnam, the bloody race riots and tragic assassinations. The focus, though, is primarily on the people and the events of that turbulent period of American history. Granted, the people and the events were unprecedented, and the era was the very definition of cultural breakdown, but the gory accounts generally don't include the federal policies that were instituted during that era that continue to contribute to our national woes.

Two 1960s policy "innovations" were especially destructive. The Flemming Rule (1960) was named for Arthur Flemming, then head of the Department of Health and Human Services, who issued an administrative ruling that states could not deny eligibility for income assistance through the AFDC [Aid to Families with Dependent Children] program on the grounds that a home was "unsuitable" because the woman's children were illegitimate. In 1968, the Supreme Court's "Man-in-the-House" rule struck down the practice of states declaring a home unsuitable (i.e., an immoral environment) if there was a man in the house not married to the mother. Thus, out-of-wedlock births and cohabitation were legitimized. In very short order, the number on welfare tripled and child poverty climbed dramatically. Unbelievably, President Bill Clinton awarded Arthur Flemming his second Presidential Medal of Freedom for his contributions to American society.

Innovation, though, does not constitute progress unless the benefits are greater than its costs—unless the intended consequences are larger than the unintended consequences. In our national history of trial and error, boom or bust, there are numerous economic and social policies that have ignored the realities of human nature with its propensities, flaws and limitations. James Madison, the father of the American Constitution, was mindful of the propensity of human nature to abuse power, and he deliberately designed a government with carefully drawn boundaries; the separation of powers between the branches of government provides essential checks and balances.

Liberals tend to ignore the need to constrain evil behavior; they see bad environmental influences as the source of evil, rather than acknowledging the existence of evil that needs to be constrained.

Results of the 1960s Rulings

So what were the results of the Flemming Rule and the "Man-in-the-House" rule? These two rulings were significant features of the "War on Poverty." Yet, the number of children living in poverty at the outset of the War on Poverty was only 13.8 percent; subsequently it climbed to a high of 22 percent before finally beginning to decline after the Welfare Reform of 1996 was enacted over the furious protests of liberals. The number of unmarried couples living together in the United States is 10 times larger today than in 1970. Many of these couples have children, despite the instability of these relationships, whose rate of dissolution is many times higher than that of married couples. Female-headed households with related children in the United States have increased a whopping 250 percent since 1970. This is important for many reasons, not the least of which is the fact that the poverty rate of children living in mother-only families is five times that of children living in married couple families.

Since Welfare Reform in 1996, the welfare caseload has declined 66 percent, and the poverty rate of children in mother-only families has dropped dramatically. Policy counts!

We are seeing dramatic results in declining teen sexual activity, pregnancies and abortions because of the [George W.] Bush Administration's commitment to abstinence education. The abortion rate per thousand teens aged 15–19 has been cut in half since 1988. Adolescent pregnancy rates have dropped from 17.5 to a low of 8.1 per thousand—note that, given the decline in the teen abortion rates, this decline in pregnancies is obviously not because of any increase in the number of pregnancies that are being aborted. These numbers are particularly dramatic among the black population. Births to black 10–14 year olds are down 56 percent. Black child poverty has declined dramatically as black unwed teen birthrates have dropped by 40 percent. Policy counts!

We are finally reversing some of the negative impact of the misguided policies of the 1960s. We MUST continue to enact policies that produce desirable outcomes.

Chapter 2

Welfare Payments Cannot Be Terminated Without a Hearing

Case Overview

Goldberg v. Kelly (1970)

In 1966 John Kelly, a twenty-nine-year-old homeless black man, was struck by a hit-and-run driver and permanently disabled. He then qualified for New York's welfare program and received a check every two weeks, which enabled him to live in a cheap hotel. After about a year his caseworker told him to move into a different hotel; Kelly was reluctant to move because he knew that hotel was filled with drug addicts and drunks. He stayed there only a few days and then moved into a friend's apartment without changing his mailing address. When he went to pick up his check he was told that his welfare benefits had been terminated. Kelly tried to reach his caseworker to find out why, but she refused to see him. Since he could not stay on with his friend without sharing expenses, he was forced to sleep on the street. A social worker he contacted was unable to talk to the caseworker either; she was simply told his case was closed.

Finally, Kelly visited the office of the Mobilization for Youth (MFY) Legal Unit, which offered legal aid to the poor. The lawyers there had been looking for a case with which they could challenge laws under which welfare benefits could be cut off as soon as a caseworker declared that the recipient was no longer eligible. "Termination was the device that the welfare department used to shake people up," MFY attorney David Drummond said. "The feeling that you can get terminated any time for anything makes you much more subservient and pliable to whatever caseworkers want." MFY persuaded Kelly to join a lawsuit that might end this policy. They also found more plaintiffs, knowing that would provide a better chance of winning than bringing a case with only one.

After long and complicated legal proceedings, the federal district court ruled on the case, finding in favor of the plaintiffs. The judges agreed that it was wrong to terminate welfare benefits without giving the recipient a chance to contest the decision. Welfare benefits, the court said, were covered by the due process clause of the Constitution's Fourteenth Amendment. In the absence of some overwhelming justification, there must be a formal hearing before payments to people in need were cut off.

Although they had won the case, the lawyers hoped it would be appealed to the Supreme Court, for what they had wanted was a ruling that would apply to the whole nation, not just New York. Moreover, they were in a race against the plaintiffs in a similar case from California, *Wheeler v. Montgomery*, which they felt was less likely to lead to a favorable ruling by the Court and might therefore result in the setting of a bad precedent. So they were happy when the City of New York, in the name of Commissioner of Social Services Jack R. Goldberg, did appeal. The Supreme Court, which considered the two cases together and decided both on the same day, ruled six to three in a landmark decision that it was unconstitutional for welfare benefits to be terminated without a prior evidentiary hearing at which the recipient was given an opportunity to confront and cross-examine witnesses.

This case is a good example of a fundamental conflict in outlook among members of the Court, a conflict that often influences the outcome of many cases. It may seem strange that when the justices of the Court are all among the finest legal scholars in America, they cannot agree among themselves about what the Constitution says. Some believe it should be interpreted strictly in accord with what the founders meant when they wrote it, while others feel its interpretation should be expanded to include conditions in the modern world.

In *Goldberg v. Kelly*, the majority took the latter position. They declared that assistance to the needy is not charity but a means of promoting the general welfare of the nation that the government should foster. Justice Hugo Black, however, dissented; he believed that the Constitution was intended to restrict the power of the government, not to interfere with whatever practices a court considers unfair or shocking. He held that the courts are not authorized to make laws—that is the role of the elected representatives of the people and should therefore be left to Congress. Nevertheless, the majority's view prevailed.

"To cut off a welfare recipient . . . without a prior hearing of some sort is unconscionable unless overwhelming considerations justify it."

Majority Opinion: The Needs of Welfare Recipients Outweigh the Government's Interest in Conserving Funds

William J. Brennan

William J. Brennan was a justice of the U.S. Supreme Court from 1956 to 1990. He was an outspoken liberal and among the Court's most influential members. In the following majority opinion in Goldberg v. Kelly, *he writes that when welfare is discontinued, only a pretermination hearing provides the recipient with the due process required by the Constitution. He points out that termination of aid pending resolution of a controversy over eligibility may deprive an eligible recipient of much-needed funds while waiting. Moreover, he asserts, public assistance is not charity but a means of promoting the general welfare of the nation, and so it serves the government's interest to provide uninterrupted benefits to those who are entitled to them. The conflicting government interest in saving money does not override this, as there are other ways of reducing costs.*

The question for decision is whether a State that terminates public assistance payments to a particular recipient without affording him the opportunity for an evidentiary hearing

William J. Brennan, majority opinion, *Goldberg v. Kelly*, U.S. Supreme Court, March 23, 1970.

prior to termination denies the recipient procedural due process in violation of the Due Process Clause of the Fourteenth Amendment.

This action was brought in the District Court for the Southern District of New York by residents of New York City receiving financial aid under the federally assisted program of Aid to Families with Dependent Children (AFDC) or under New York State's general Home Relief program. Their complaint alleged that the New York State and New York City officials administering these programs terminated, or were about to terminate, such aid without prior notice and hearing, thereby denying them due process of law. At the time the suits were filed, there was no requirement of prior notice or hearing of any kind before termination of financial aid. However, the State and city adopted procedures for notice and hearing after the suits were brought, and the plaintiffs, appellees here, then challenged the constitutional adequacy of those procedures. . . .

Pursuant to subdivision (b), the New York City Department of Social Services promulgated Procedure No. 68-18. A caseworker who has doubts about the recipient's continued eligibility must first discuss them with the recipient. If the caseworker concludes that the recipient is no longer eligible, he recommends termination of aid to a unit supervisor. If the latter concurs, he sends the recipient a letter stating the reasons for proposing to terminate aid and notifying him that, within seven days, he may request that a higher official review the record, and may support the request with a written statement, prepared personally or with the aid of an attorney or other person. If the reviewing official affirms the determination of ineligibility, aid is stopped immediately and the recipient is informed by letter of the reasons for the action. Appellees' challenge to this procedure emphasizes the absence of any provisions for the personal appearance of the recipient before the reviewing official, for oral presentation of evidence, and for confrontation and cross-examination of adverse witnesses. However, the letter does inform the recipient that he may request a post-termination "fair hearing." This is a proceeding before an independent state hearing officer at which the recipient may appear personally, offer oral evidence, confront and cross-examine the witnesses against him, and have a record made of the hearing. If the recipient prevails at the "fair hearing," he is paid all funds erroneously withheld. A recipient whose aid is not restored by a "fair hearing" decision may have judicial review. The recipient is so notified.

The constitutional issue to be decided, therefore, is the narrow one: whether the Due Process Clause requires that the recipient be afforded an evidentiary hearing *before* the termination of benefits. The District Court held that only a pre-termination evidentiary hearing would satisfy the constitutional command, and rejected the argument of the state and city officials that the combination of the post-termination "fair hearing" with the informal pre-termination review disposed of all due process claims. The court said:

> While post-termination review is relevant, there is one overpowering fact which controls here. By hypothesis, a welfare recipient is destitute, without funds or assets. . . . Suffice it to say that to cut off a welfare recipient in the face of . . . "brutal need" without a prior hearing of some sort is unconscionable unless overwhelming considerations justify it.

The court rejected the argument that the need to protect the public's tax revenues supplied the requisite "overwhelming consideration."

> Against the justified desire to protect public funds must be weighed the individual's overpowering need in this unique situation not to be wrongfully deprived of assistance. . . . While the problem of additional expense must be kept in mind, it does not justify denying a hearing meeting the ordinary standards of due process. Under all the circumstances,

we hold that due process requires an adequate hearing before termination of welfare benefits, and the fact that there is a later constitutionally fair proceeding does not alter the result. . . .

Public Assistance Is Not Mere Charity

Appellant does not contend that procedural due process is not applicable to the termination of welfare benefits. Such benefits are a matter of statutory entitlement for persons qualified to receive them. Their termination involves state action that adjudicates important rights. The constitutional challenge cannot be answered by an argument that public assistance benefits are "a 'privilege,' and not a 'right.'" . . .

It is true, of course, that some governmental benefits may be administratively terminated without affording the recipient a pre-termination evidentiary hearing. But we agree with the District Court that, when welfare is discontinued, only a pre-termination evidentiary hearing provides the recipient with procedural due process. For qualified recipients, welfare provides the means to obtain essential food, clothing, housing, and medical care. Thus, the crucial factor in this context—a factor not present in the case of the blacklisted government contractor, the discharged government employee, the taxpayer denied a tax exemption, or virtually anyone else whose governmental entitlements are ended—is that termination of aid pending resolution of a controversy over eligibility may deprive an eligible recipient of the very means by which to live while he waits. Since he lacks independent resources, his situation becomes immediately desperate. His need to concentrate upon finding the means for daily subsistence, in turn, adversely affects his ability to seek redress from the welfare bureaucracy.

Moreover, important governmental interests are promoted by affording recipients a pre-termination evidentiary hearing. From its founding, the Nation's basic commitment has been to foster the dignity and wellbeing of all persons within its borders. We have come to recognize that forces not within the control of the poor contribute to their poverty. This perception, against the background of our traditions, has significantly influenced the development of the contemporary public assistance system. Welfare, by meeting the basic demands of subsistence, can help bring within the reach of the poor the same opportunities that are available to others to participate meaningfully in the life of the community. At the same time, welfare guards against the societal malaise that may flow from a widespread sense of unjustified frustration and insecurity. Public assistance, then, is not mere charity, but a means to "promote the general Welfare, and secure the Blessings of Liberty to ourselves and our Posterity." The same governmental interests that counsel the provision of welfare, counsel as well its uninterrupted provision to those eligible to receive it; pretermination evidentiary hearings are indispensable to that end.

Rights Outweigh Costs

Appellant does not challenge the force of these considerations but argues that they are outweighed by countervailing governmental interests in conserving fiscal and administrative resources. These interests, the argument goes, justify the delay of any evidentiary hearing until after discontinuance of the grants. Summary adjudication protects the public fisc [treasury] by stopping payments promptly upon discovery of reason to believe that a recipient is no longer eligible. Since most terminations are accepted without challenge, summary adjudication also conserves both the fisc and administrative time and energy by reducing the number of evidentiary hearings actually held.

We agree with the District Court, however, that these governmental interests are not overriding in the welfare context. The requirement of a prior hearing doubtless involves some greater expense, and the benefits paid to ineligible recipients pending decision at the hearing probably cannot he recouped, since these recipients are likely to be judgment-proof. But the State is not without weapons to minimize these increased costs. Much of the drain on fiscal and administrative resources can be reduced by developing procedures for prompt pre-termination hearings and by skillful use of personnel and facilities. Indeed, the very provision for a post-termination evidentiary hearing in New York's Home Relief program is itself cogent evidence that the State recognizes the primacy of the public interest in correct eligibility determinations, and therefore in the provision of procedural safeguards. Thus, the interest of the eligible recipient in uninterrupted receipt of public assistance, coupled with the State's interest that his payments not be erroneously terminated, clearly outweighs the State's competing concern to prevent any increase in its fiscal and administrative burdens. As the District Court correctly concluded,

> [t]he stakes are simply too high for the welfare recipient, and the possibility for honest error or irritable misjudgment too great, to allow termination of aid without giving the recipient a chance, if he so desires, to be fully informed of the case against him so that he may contest its basis and produce evidence in rebuttal. . . .

We wish to add that we, no less than the dissenters, recognize the importance of not imposing upon the States or the Federal Government in this developing field of law any procedural requirements beyond those demanded by rudimentary due process.

The Right to Be Heard

"The fundamental requisite of due process of law is the opportunity to be heard" *Grannis v. Ordean*. . . . The opportunity to be heard must be tailored to the capacities and circumstances of those who are to be heard. It is not enough that a welfare recipient may present his position to the decisionmaker in writing or second-hand through his caseworker. Written submissions are an unrealistic option for most recipients, who lack the educational attainment necessary to write effectively and who cannot obtain professional assistance. Moreover, written submissions do not afford the flexibility of oral presentations; they do not permit the recipient to mold his argument to the issues the decisionmaker appears to regard as important. Particularly where credibility and veracity are at issue, as they must be in many termination proceedings, written submissions are a wholly unsatisfactory basis for decision. The second-hand presentation to the decisionmaker by the caseworker has its own deficiencies; since the caseworker usually gathers the facts upon which the charge of ineligibility rests, the presentation of the recipient's side of the controversy cannot safely be left to him. Therefore, a recipient must be allowed to state his position orally. Informal procedures will suffice; in this context, due process does not require a particular order of proof or mode of offering evidence.

In almost every setting where important decisions turn on questions of fact, due process requires an opportunity to confront and cross-examine adverse witnesses. What we said in *Greene v. McElroy* is particularly pertinent here:

> Certain principles have remained relatively immutable in our jurisprudence. One of these is that, where governmental action seriously injures an individual, and the reasonableness of the action depends on fact findings, the evidence used to prove the Government's case must be disclosed to the individual so that he has an opportunity to show that it is untrue. While this is important in the case of documentary evidence, it is even more important where the evidence consists of the testimony of individuals whose memory might be faulty or who, in fact, might be perjurers or persons motivated by malice, vindictiveness, intolerance, prejudice, or jealousy. We have formalized these protections in the requirements of confrontation and cross-examination. They have ancient roots. They find expression in the Sixth

Amendment. . . . This Court has been zealous to protect these rights from erosion. It has spoken out not only in criminal cases, . . . but also in all types of cases where administrative . . . actions were under scrutiny.

Welfare recipients must therefore be given an opportunity to confront and cross-examine the witnesses relied on by the department.

"The right to be heard would be in many cases, of little avail if it did not comprehend the right to be heard by counsel" [*Powell v. Alabama*]. We do not say that counsel must be provided at the pre-termination hearing, but only that the recipient must be allowed to retain an attorney if he so desires. . . .

Finally, the decisionmaker's conclusion as to a recipient's eligibility must rest solely on the legal rules and evidence adduced at the hearing. To demonstrate compliance with this elementary requirement, the decisionmaker should state the reasons for his determination and indicate the evidence he relied on, though his statement need not amount to a full opinion, or even formal findings of fact and conclusions of law. And, of course, an impartial decisionmaker is essential. We agree with the District Court that prior involvement in some aspects of a case will not necessarily bar a welfare official from acting as a decisionmaker. He should not, however, have participated in making the determination under review.

> "Today's result does not depend on the language of the Constitution . . . but solely on the collective judgment of the majority as to what would be a fair and humane procedure."

Dissenting Opinion: Nothing in the Constitution Gives Judges the Power to Make Laws

Hugo Black

Hugo Black was a justice of the Supreme Court from 1937 until 1971 and is considered one of the most influential members of the Court of the twentieth century. He believed in a literal interpretation of the Constitution, and in the following dissenting opinion in Goldberg v. Kelly *argues that the Court should not alter the meaning of the due process clause in order to bring about change in laws it considers unfair. He would not object to the majority decision if it were made by the legislative branch of government, he says, but it is not appropriate for courts to make laws, which under the Constitution is the function of legislators. Furthermore, he does not believe the Court's decision will help the needy, because if the government cannot stop anyone's welfare benefits until after a long appeal, fewer people will be added to the welfare rolls in the first place. He declares that experiments with welfare should be left to Congress and state legislatures instead of being frozen into the Constitution.*

Hugo Black, dissenting opinion, *Goldberg v. Kelly*, U.S. Supreme Court, March 23, 1970.

In the last half century, the United States, along with many, perhaps most, other nations of the world, has moved far toward becoming a welfare state, that is, a nation that, for one reason or another, taxes its most affluent people to help support, feed, clothe, and shelter its less fortunate citizens. The result is that, today, more than nine million men, women, and children in the United States receive some kind of state or federally financed public assistance in the form of allowances or gratuities, generally paid them periodically, usually by the week, month, or quarter. Since these gratuities are paid on the basis of need, the list of recipients is not static, and some people go off the lists and others are added from time to time. These ever-changing lists put a constant administrative burden on government, and it certainly could not have reasonably anticipated that this burden would include the additional procedural expense imposed by the Court today.

The dilemma of the ever-increasing poor in the midst of constantly growing affluence presses upon us, and must inevitably be met within the framework of our democratic constitutional government if our system is to survive as such. It was largely to escape just such pressing economic problems and attendant government repression that people from Europe, Asia, and other areas settled this country and formed our Nation. Many of those settlers had personally suffered from persecutions of various kinds, and wanted to get away from governments that had unrestrained powers to make life miserable for their citizens. It was for this reason, or so I believe, that, on reaching these new lands, the early settlers undertook to curb their governments by confining their powers within written boundaries, which eventually became written constitutions. They wrote their basic charters, as nearly as men's collective wisdom could do so, as to proclaim to their people and their officials an emphatic command [as similarly expressed in the Tenth Amendment] that: "Thus far and no farther shall you go, and where we neither delegate powers to you, nor prohibit your exercise of them, we the people are left free."

Representatives of the people of the Thirteen Original Colonies spent long, hot months in the summer of 1787 in Philadelphia, Pennsylvania, creating a government of limited powers. They divided it into three departments—Legislative, Judicial, and Executive. The Judicial Department was to have no part whatever in making any laws. In fact, proposals looking to vesting some power in the Judiciary to take part in the legislative process and veto laws were offered, considered, and rejected by the Constitutional Convention. In my judgment, there is not one word, phrase, or sentence from the beginning to the end of the Constitution from which it can be inferred that judges were granted any such legislative power. True, *Marbury v. Madison*, held, and properly, I think, that courts must be the final interpreters of the Constitution, and I recognize that the holding can provide an opportunity to slide imperceptibly into constitutional amendment and law-making. But when federal judges use this judicial power for legislative purposes, I think they wander out of their field of vested powers and transgress into the area constitutionally assigned to the Congress and the people. That is precisely what I believe the Court is doing in this case. Hence, my dissent.

Not Based on the Constitution

The more than a million names on the relief rolls in New York, and the more than nine million names on the rolls of all the 50 States, were not put there at random. The names are there because state welfare officials believed that those people were eligible for assistance. Probably, in the officials' haste to make out the lists, many names were put there erroneously in order to alleviate immediate suffering, and undoubtedly some people are drawing relief who are not entitled under the law to do so. Doubtless some draw relief checks from time to time who know they are not eligible, either because they are not actually in need or for some other reason. Many of those who thus draw undeserved gratuities are without sufficient property to enable the government to collect back from them any money they wrongfully receive. But the Court today holds that it would violate the Due Process Clause of the Fourteenth Amendment to stop paying those people weekly or monthly allowances unless the government first affords them a full "evidentiary hearing," even though welfare officials are persuaded that the recipients are not rightfully entitled to receive a penny under the law. In other words, although some recipients might be on the lists for payment wholly because of deliberate fraud on their part, the Court holds that the government is helpless, and must continue, until after an evidentiary hearing, to pay money that it does not owe, never has owed, and never could owe. I do not believe there is any provision in our Constitution that should thus paralyze the government's efforts to protect itself against making payments to people who are not entitled to them.

Particularly do I not think that the Fourteenth Amendment should be given such an unnecessarily broad construction. That Amendment came into being primarily to protect Negroes from discrimination, and while some of its language can and does protect others, all know that the chief purpose behind it was to protect ex-slaves. The Court, however, relies upon the Fourteenth Amendment, and, in effect, says that failure of the government to pay a promised charitable installment to an individual deprives that individual of *his own property* in violation of the Due Process Clause of the Fourteenth Amendment. It somewhat strains credulity to say that the government's promise of charity to an individual is property belonging to that individual when the government denies that the individual is honestly entitled to receive such a payment.

I would have little, if any, objection to the majority's decision in this case if it were written as the report of the House

Committee on Education and Labor, but, as an opinion ostensibly resting on the language of the Constitution, I find it woefully deficient. Once the verbiage is pared away, it is obvious that this Court today adopts the views of the District Court "that to cut off a welfare recipient in the face of . . . 'brutal need' without a prior hearing of some sort is unconscionable," and therefore, says the Court, unconstitutional. The majority reaches this result by a process of weighing "the recipient's interest in avoiding" the termination of welfare benefits against "the governmental interest in summary adjudication." Today's balancing act requires a "pre-termination evidentiary hearing," yet there is nothing that indicates what tomorrow's balance will be. Although the majority attempts to bolster its decision with limited quotations from prior cases, it is obvious that today's result does not depend on the language of the Constitution itself or the principles of other decisions, but solely on the collective judgment of the majority as to what would be a fair and humane procedure in this case.

Court Misinterpreted Due Process

This decision is thus only another variant of the view often expressed by some members of this Court that the Due Process Clause forbids any conduct that a majority of the Court believes "unfair," "indecent," or "shocking to their consciences." Neither these words nor any like them appear anywhere in the Due Process Clause. If they did, they would leave the majority of Justices free to hold any conduct unconstitutional that they should conclude on their own to be unfair or shocking to them. Had the drafters of the Due Process Clause meant to leave judges such ambulatory power to declare laws unconstitutional, the chief value of a written constitution, as the Founders saw it, would have been lost. In fact, if that view of due process is correct, the Due Process Clause could easily swallow up all other parts of the Constitution. And, truly, the

Constitution would always be "what the judges say it is" at a given moment, not what the Founders wrote into the document. A written constitution, designed to guarantee protection against governmental abuses, including those of judges, must have written standards that mean something definite and have an explicit content. I regret very much to be compelled to say that the Court today makes a drastic and dangerous departure from a Constitution written to control and limit the government and the judges, and moves toward a constitution designed to be no more and no less than what the judges of a particular social and economic philosophy declare, on the one hand, to be fair, or, on the other hand, to be shocking and unconscionable.

The procedure required today as a matter of constitutional law finds no precedent in our legal system. Reduced to its simplest terms, the problem in this case is similar to that frequently encountered when two parties have an ongoing legal relationship that requires one party to make periodic payments to the other. Often the situation arises where the party "owing" the money stops paying it and justifies his conduct by arguing that the recipient is not legally entitled to payment. The recipient can, of course, disagree and go to court to compel payment. But I know of no situation in our legal system in which the person alleged to owe money to another is required by law to continue making payments to a judgment-proof claimant without the benefit of any security or bond to insure that these payments can be recovered if he wins his legal argument. Yet today's decision in no way obligates the welfare recipient to pay back any benefits wrongfully received during the pre-termination evidentiary hearings or post any bond, and, in all "fairness," it could not do so. These recipients are, by definition, too poor to post a bond or to repay the benefits that, as the majority assumes, must be spent as received to insure survival.

No Benefit to the Poor

The Court apparently feels that this decision will benefit the poor and needy. In my judgment, the eventual result will be just the opposite. While today's decision requires only an administrative, evidentiary hearing, the inevitable logic of the approach taken will lead to constitutionally imposed, time-consuming delays of a full adversary process of administrative and judicial review. In the next case, the welfare recipients are bound to argue that cutting off benefits before judicial review of the agency's decision is also a denial of due process. Since, by hypothesis, termination of aid at that point may still "deprive an eligible recipient of the very means by which to live while he waits," I would be surprised if the weighing process did not compel the conclusion that termination without full judicial review would be unconscionable. After all, at each step, as the majority seems to feel, the issue is only one of weighing the government's pocketbook against the actual survival of the recipient, and surely that balance must always tip in favor of the individual. Similarly today's decision requires only the opportunity to have the benefit of counsel at the administrative hearing, but it is difficult to believe that the same reasoning process would not require the appointment of counsel, for otherwise the right to counsel is a meaningless one, since these people are too poor to hire their own advocates. Thus, the end result of today's decision may well be that the government, once it decides to give welfare benefits, cannot reverse that decision until the recipient has had the benefits of full administrative and Judicial review, including, of course, the opportunity to present his case to this Court. Since this process will usually entail a delay of several years, the inevitable result of such a constitutionally imposed burden will be that the government will not put a claimant on the rolls initially until it has made an exhaustive investigation to determine his eligibility. While this Court will perhaps have insured that no needy person will be taken off the rolls without a full "due process" proceeding, it will also have insured that many will never get on the rolls, or at least that they will remain destitute during the lengthy proceedings followed to determine initial eligibility.

For the foregoing reasons, I dissent from the Court's holding. The operation of a welfare state is a new experiment for our Nation. For this reason, among others, I feel that new experiments in carrying out a welfare program should not be frozen into our constitutional structure. They should be left, as are other legislative determinations, to the Congress and the legislatures that the people elect to make our laws.

"[Justice Black] was not open to arguments that the definition of property under the due process clause must be revised in light of contemporary government's dealings with its beneficiaries."

The Supreme Court Justices Had Conflicting Views of Due Process in *Goldberg v. Kelly*

Martha F. Davis

Martha F. Davis is a professor and associate dean at Northeastern University School of Law. She received the Reginald Heber Smith Award for distinguished scholarship on the subject of equal access to justice for her book Brutal Need: Lawyers and the Welfare Rights Movement, *from which the following excerpt is taken. In it, she describes the discussions that the Supreme Court justices had when they were deciding* Goldberg v. Kelly. *It was clear from the beginning that they were divided, she contends, but even among those who sided with the majority there were differences, and compromises had to be made in preparing the final draft of the opinion. All three dissenters wrote separate opinions. Hugo Black felt so strongly about his that he stayed awake at night writing it in his mind. He believed that the Court should not change the original intent of the Constitution by making decisions that should be left to Congress.*

The postargument conference on *Wheeler v. Montgomery* and *Goldberg v. Kelly* [similar cases considered together by the Supreme Court] was held [October 17, 1969]. Sitting around a table without their usual accoutrements—robes and clerks—in order of seniority each justice stated his position on each case heard during the week. In addition, the justices discussed the progress of opinion-writing on previously decided cases.

[Warren] Burger, sitting at the head of the table, went first. He voted to reverse [circuit court judge Wilfred] Feinberg's decision and uphold the city's procedures.

As the senior associate justice on the Court, Justice [Hugo] Black sat opposite Burger at the conference table and spoke immediately after the chief justice. He also voted to reverse.

[William] Douglas followed, expressing his view that welfare benefits were a "species of property" and voting to affirm the lower court.

[John Marshall] Harlan spoke next, also voting to affirm Feinberg. "This is not a gratuity," he told his colleagues. "It is an entitlement or right under the federal program and in state programs . . . a vested right as long as the state chooses to give it." He emphasized, however, that the Court's approach must be flexible in determining what type of hearing might be required. [William] Brennan also voted to affirm, as did [Thurgood] Marshall.

"I am more with John than with the two Bills," explained [Byron] White when his turn came. "The impact here is so severe that the balance should be cast for a full hearing before termination."

Finally, [Potter] Stewart voted to reverse the three-judge court while specifically rejecting Black's view that welfare was not a form of property. "I don't think the distinction between a vested right and a gratuity is significant as to what requirements of due process obtain," he said. But "the totality of procedures here . . . satisfies due process."

Burger spoke again. "We should let these cases alone," he advised. "It's like pulling up radishes to see how they are growing and ending up with no radishes."

Because he was in the minority in the *Goldberg* and *Wheeler* cases, Burger indicated that Douglas, the senior member of the majority, should assign the opinions. Sensing a close vote, which might require some compromise to keep White and Harlan in the majority, Douglas gave the task of writing the opinions to Brennan. . . .

Drafting Opinions

Brennan's law clerks for the 1969 term were Richard Cooper, a Harvard Law School graduate, and Taylor Reveley, a Southerner from the University of Virginia Law School. Two other law clerks, Douglas Poe and Marshall Moriarty, were chosen by Burger and assigned to Brennan's staff

Brennan typically prepared himself for oral arguments by reading the parties' briefs. After an argument, he might ask one of his clerks to help research a particular point of law prior to the Friday conference at which the justices reviewed the week's cases. Following the conference, Brennan returned to his chambers, preceded by a messenger drawing a large cart loaded with the books on which the justice had relied in reaching his decision. According to Reveley, "These books, along with his notes of the conference, would go to his clerks, and we would get to work." It was the clerks' job to write the first draft of Brennan's opinions, which he would then review and edit. Because there was not a clear division of labor in Brennan's chambers—each clerk chipped in as he had the time—all of the clerks worked on various aspects of drafting the *Wheeler* and *Goldberg* opinions. . . .

By the end of November the justices were drafting opinions and choosing sides. Burger circulated a memo indicating that he intended to dissent in both *Wheeler* and *Goldberg* and that he would await Black's opinion. At the same time, Burger sent Black a copy of a draft dissent in which he worked out in more detail his "radish" theory.

"Hugo," the draft began, "here are some 'thoughts while shaving'" on the New York and California welfare cases. "The states and the federal agencies should be permitted to experiment rather than being forced into a mold which may or may not be suited either to expanding or contracting benefits. At least one generation of welfare recipients has grown up without the procedural safeguards now found to be imperative under the Constitution. . . . If the history of the cost and complexity of the administrative processes and judicial review, as we have seen it since the 1930s, is repeated and this new layer of procedural protection is subsidized, as it must be, by the public treasury, the zealous advocates for welfare claimants may be on the way to 'killing the golden goose.'"

Brennan's first draft of the *Goldberg* opinion was circulated to the Court on November 24, 1969, with a second draft following on November 28. Although the initial outline of the opinion prepared by Reveley chronicled the story of each welfare recipient involved in the case, the circulated version focused on two representative plaintiffs, Altagrazia Guzman and Juan DeJesus. The clerk also wrote at length about the nature of poverty, calling it "largely a product of impersonal forces." Welfare, he wrote, was the "treatment of a disorder inherent in our society. Government has an overriding interest in providing welfare to the eligible, both to help maintain the dignity and well-being of a large segment of the population and to guard against the societal malaise that may flow from a widespread sense of unwarranted frustration and insecurity."

The exposition was included in the first draft circulated to the Court, but after Harlan labeled the discussion "offensive" and White flatly refused to accept it, the passage was excised. In its place, Brennan crafted a paragraph reflecting White's view that welfare is not a societal obligation but a benefit given to help the poor participate fully in society.

The second draft also addressed the dissents Brennan anticipated. In an attempt to allay Black's fears, Brennan specifically stated that in *Goldberg v. Kelly* "we do not consider whether a recipient has a substantive due process right to receive welfare" but limit consideration to the requirements of procedural due process. Brennan then asserted, citing Charles Reich's work, that "it may be realistic today to regard welfare entitlements as more like 'property' than a 'gratuity.'" Thus, wrote Brennan, welfare benefits could no longer be considered charity, and the requirements of the due process clause must apply to their administration. . . .

Marshall and Douglas joined Brennan's opinions in *Wheeler* and *Goldberg* immediately. White followed on December 2.

Black's Dissent

Black, however, was stirred after reading the majority's preliminary opinion. His wife, Elizabeth, recorded in her diary for December 4, 1969, that "Hugo couldn't sleep. He was extremely exhilarated. He had a dissent rolling around in his mind (to Bill Brennan's opinion saying a hearing is due to anyone severed from Relief Roll as a constitutional right). Hugo was like other years when he would get on fire about an opinion."

The next day, Black was still agitated. "He woke up at 3:00 A.M.," wrote Elizabeth Black, "and got up and talked. He said his mind was racing and he was 'writing' an opinion in his mind. It must be, said he, the [storied Supreme Court justice Oliver Wendell] Holmes-type opinion—short, classic, citing no authorities—about 'I am fearful that the Court goes farther and farther on the Due Process Clause,' in regard to a case whereby if anyone ever gets his name on the welfare rolls, he is entitled constitutionally to a hearing before he is removed. Hugo still couldn't sleep at 4:00, and so he got up and took a drink." . . .

Black's former clerk, Charles Reich, wrote in a 1962 tribute to his mentor that constitutional principles must move "in the same direction and at the same rate as the rest of society." Black responded to Reich in his dissent in *Griswold v. Connecticut* in 1965, in which the majority of the Court found that individuals have a constitutional privacy right to make personal decisions regarding contraception. Black wrote, "I realize that many good and able men have eloquently spoken and written, sometimes in rhapsodical strains, about the duty of this Court to keep the Constitution in tune with the times. The idea is that the Constitution must be changed from time to time and that this Court is charged with a duty to make those changes. For myself, I must with all deference reject that philosophy. The Constitution makers knew the need for change and provided for it. Amendments suggested by the people's elected representatives can be submitted. . . . That method of change was good for our Fathers, and being somewhat old-fashioned I must add it is good enough for me." Later, while reading Charles Reich's 1970 book *The Greening of America*, Black announced that he was a "Consciousness I" man, described in Reich's book as one who "is unwilling or unable to comprehend the transformation of America" from the nineteenth to twentieth centuries.

By 1969 Black viewed the Constitution as a document that definitively identified and limited potential government excesses. He was not open to arguments that the definition of property under the due process clause must be revised in light of contemporary government's dealings with its beneficiaries. . . .

Black wrote his dissent during the next few weeks. It began with a review of the Constitutional Convention and the structure of government intended by the Constitution's framers. "The judicial department was to have no part whatsoever in making any laws," wrote Black. The majority of the Court, however, "says that failure of the government to pay a promised charitable installment to an individual deprives that individual of *his property*, and thus violates the due process clause of the Fourteenth Amendment." According to Black, the majority's opinion was tantamount to substantive due process: "This is another variant of the view often expressed by some members of the Court that the due process clause forbids any conduct that a majority of the Court believes is 'unfair,' 'indecent,' or 'shocking to the conscience.'

"Had the Constitution meant by the due process clause to leave judges such ambulatory power to declare laws unconstitutional," Black argued, "the chief value of a written constitution as the Founders saw would have been lost. In fact, if that view of due process is right, the due process clause would swallow up all other parts of the Constitution."

Black concluded with an approving nod to Burger's dissent. "The function of a welfare state," he wrote, "is a new experiment for our nation. For this reason, among others, I agree with the Chief Justice that new experiments in carrying on such a state should not be frozen into our Constitutional structure, but should be left as are other legislative determinations, to the Congress which the people elect to make our laws." Black completed the draft dissent during his midwinter Florida vacation and mailed it from Miami. . . .

As one of Black's law clerks later explained his employer's vehement opposition to the majority opinion, "The Justice has become increasingly concerned that various members of the Court have let their views run wild. Thus he's eager to take an unusually strict constructionist—The Words—approach to attempt to pull the Court back into line. A part of his eagerness stems from an awareness that each year may be his last as an active Justice."

Final Revisions

On December 11, Brennan received a letter from Harlan concerning the draft majority opinion. The two justices had already talked about their points of disagreement, and the letter simply set them out formally. "There are some things in your opinion," Harlan wrote, "to which I would not wish to subscribe, and in order to avoid any separate writing on my part (which I would much prefer not to have to do) I thought I would put such matters to you for consideration."

Harlan's objections were mostly minor. He questioned the term "trial-type hearing," which he believed was not sufficiently precise. Harlan suggested that "evidentiary hearing" be used instead.

Harlan also asserted that fair hearings should be limited to cases involving factual disputes—for example, whether the recipient was employed—as opposed to those involving such statutory interpretations as whether a state welfare regulation conformed to federal requirements. . . .

"If you can see your way clear to meeting my suggestions," he concluded, "I am prepared to join your opinion, which I think is a very good one, subject to further suggestions, or possibly some separate writing, after the dissent makes its appearance." . . .

Brennan replied to Harlan in a letter dated December 15. He agreed to revise his draft opinion based on Harlan's comments, asking Harlan to compromise only on his insistence that due process did not necessarily require a full hearing when purely legal issues were at stake. Brennan asked simply that Harlan agree to leave the issue open, to be resolved in a future case.

On February 19, 1970, Harlan wrote to accept Brennan's compromise, adding that "I have decided to do no separate writing in either case myself." Harlan also asked that Brennan consider adding a final paragraph to his opinion, stating that "in reaching these conclusions, we wish to add that we, no less than the minority, recognize the importance of not imposing upon the states or the federal government in this developing field of the law any procedural requirements beyond those demanded by rudimentary due process." Harlan added that "I am content to leave this last suggestion in your hands, but for myself would consider it an appropriate thought to add." Brennan added the sentence to the opinion following his discussion of the minimal procedural safeguards necessary to ensure due process.

On February 17 Stewart circulated his one-sentence dissent from Brennan's opinion. "The question for me is a close one," he wrote, but "I do not believe that the procedures that New York and California now follow in terminating welfare payments are violative of the United States Constitution."

The opinions were announced on March 23. . . . The majority opinion expressly rejected the argument that the financial concerns of New York City outweighed the rights of recipients. Finally, the opinion spelled out the basic requirements of due process: a right to an appeal before an independent adjudicator, a right to present oral evidence, and a right to cross-examine witnesses.

Black, Stewart, and Burger wrote separate dissents, substantially the same as those they had circulated.

> "The high court ruling is expected to
> have far-reaching effects . . . in the na-
> tional welfare system."

Goldberg v. Kelly Will Have Far-Reaching Effects

Carol Honsa

Carol Honsa was a staff writer for the Washington Post. *In the
following article she reports that welfare officials and recipients
in Washington, D.C., are praising the Supreme Court's decision
in* Goldberg v. Kelly *because, although in the District of Columbia there was already a right to a hearing before welfare benefits
could be stopped, the ruling will have far-reaching effects elsewhere. But some people, she says, believe the Court did not go
far enough and should have required the free appointment of
lawyers for welfare recipients who request a hearing, as is done
in some places through organizations such as the Legal Aid Society. On the other hand, Honsa explains, some are worried that
the right to payments during appeals will be abused by welfare
recipients who merely want to prolong benefits to which they are
no longer entitled.*

District of Columbia welfare officials and organized relief
recipients yesterday praised a Supreme Court decision
giving welfare clients the right to a full hearing before their
benefits can be reduced or stopped.

While city welfare clients have had that right since 1968,
the high court ruling is expected to have far-reaching effects
elsewhere in the national welfare system. In nearly all states

besides the District and Mississippi, disputed welfare payments are, in effect, cut back first and restored later if the client wins an appeal.

But city welfare rights leader Sarah McPherson said the court had not gone far enough in broadening relief clients' rights because it stopped short of requiring free appointed lawyers for recipients involved in appeals.

District Deputy Welfare Director Albert P. Russo warned that the decision may mean months of extra relief benefits for recipients clearly not eligible for them.

Welfare rights militants say the present system in most states has meant months of hardship for aggrieved relief-clients who get reduced or no incomes while their appeals are heard.

The high court decision will have little impact in the District of Columbia, where the City Council has required full payments to relief clients pending the outcome of hearings in disputed cases. The Council passed this requirement in September, 1968, to protect city welfare clients from arbitrary or capricious cutbacks or terminations of their monthly checks.

Under court order, Mississippi also continues relief payments until appeals are decided, according to a U.S. Department of Health, Education and Welfare [HEW] spokesman.

Maryland relief clients receive retroactive payments if a hearing determines that their benefits were wrongly cut off or reduced, an official of the Maryland Department of Social Services said. This was the system in Washington until the City Council made the 1968 change.

Legal Aid in Hearings

HEW now permits, but does not require, states to pay out full relief benefits until appeals are decided. But it has already issued a regulation requiring all states to pay full benefits in appeals beginning July 1 [1970].

A HEW spokesman said the agency may update the July 1 deadline after studying the Supreme Court decision.

The HEW regulation, however, goes beyond the court decision in requiring state welfare agencies to make lawyers available to recipients who want them in hearings beginning July 1. HEW says this can be done through existing legal aid programs where available.

The D.C. welfare department does not provide lawyers, but most relief clients bringing appeals are represented by the Neighborhood Legal Services Program, the Legal Aid Society or private lawyers. Hearings without lawyers representing welfare clients are "uncommon" here, Russo said.

He noted that the number of hearings had drastically increased since 1965, when the antipoverty legal service program began here. Recipients filed 191 requests for the so-called "fair hearings" in fiscal 1969 and 98 from July through February of this fiscal year.

Mrs. McPherson, head of the 1,200-member D.C. Family Rights Organization, said the Supreme Court should have required legal aid for recipients involved in hearings across the nation. Lawyers for welfare departments "say things the welfare recipient might not understand because they use some of those big words," she said.

Some May Abuse Right to Hearing

Russo said the right to full relief payments during appeals can be abused by recipients trying to prolong benefits to which they are no longer entitled. Under the broadly written City Council regulation, a welfare mother whose child has died can appeal the reduction of her check and continue getting aid intended for the dead child for months until she loses her appeal, he said.

The Supreme Court left open the question whether less than a full hearing would be constitutional in cases where no factual issues are in dispute.

> "It is reassuring that the most powerful lawyers in the country can still recognize the importance of the everyday problems affecting the lives of ordinary citizens."

Goldberg v. Kelly Has Lasting Significance

Randy Lee

Randy Lee is a professor of law at the Widener University School of Law in Harrisburg, Pennsylvania. In the following viewpoint he discusses William Brennan's opinion in Goldberg v. Kelly, *pointing out that unlike Brennan's other opinions, it does not include details about the human side of the case. It is strange, he says, that Brennan omitted information that was in the District Court's opinion about the impact of the loss of welfare benefits on the lives of the people involved. Lee then points out that in the twenty-five years between the* Goldberg *decision and the time he is writing, courts have not stuck to the decision's analysis of the due process clause of the Constitution, and he speculates about whether the case should still be considered an important one. He concludes that it should be, because its impact on other cases shows that the Supreme Court justices have remained committed to finding solutions to the problems of interpreting the Constitution when faced with ordinary people's problems.*

[I]n *Goldberg v. Kelly*], writing for the majority, [William] Brennan determined that "the Due Process Clause requires that the recipient be afforded an evidentiary hearing

Randy Lee, "Twenty-five Years After *Goldberg v. Kelly*: Traveling from the Right Spot on the Wrong Road to the Wrong Place," *Capital University Law Review*, vol. 23, 1994, pp. 880–87, 921–1002. Copyright © 1994, Randy Lee. Reproduced by permission.

'before' the termination of benefits." In the opinion, Brennan found a property interest and a lack of sufficient due process protection through a test that tended to blur the property and due process elements. Clearly, the test he applied did not combine these two elements as the Court had in *Cafeteria Workers v. McElroy* but his analyses of the two requirements did overlap within the opinion. This overlap may have contributed to subsequent confusion.

This problem, however, seems trivial in light of other questions raised by Brennan's *Goldberg* opinion. First, both colleagues and commentators considered Brennan to write opinions which were particularly sensitive to the human side of his cases, but in *Goldberg* he omitted the relevant facts that would have reflected this sensitivity. Chief Justice Earl Warren, for example, said of Brennan, "His belief in the dignity of human beings—all human beings is unbounded. He also believes that without such dignity men cannot be free. These beliefs are apparent in the warp and woof of all his opinions." Similarly, Dean Erwin Griswold of Harvard said of Brennan the following:

> [His] approach is not overtly philosophic. He is interested in people as people. He is concerned with the impact of the law on the individual before the Court, and he is thoroughly aware of the influence which the Court's decision will have on the conduct of countless others not before the Court.

Normally, Brennan's opinions bore out these observations as the opinions would reveal numerous details about the people involved and the circumstances in which they found themselves. . . .

Puzzling Omissions

To some degree, Brennan brought this approach to his writing of *Goldberg*. At the outset, he was meticulous in describing how the State had failed to resolve underlying questions of eligibility for terminated recipients even though the State resumed the payment of benefits in response to the lawsuit. Ironically however, when Brennan reached those parts of the opinion where specific facts could have helped the reader understand new legal concepts, like "participate meaningfully" and "societal malaise," or get a sense of the parameters of subjective factors, like "brutal need," he omitted facts entirely. Not only does this omission deny the reader facts necessary to understand what Brennan was talking about legally, but it also denies the reader the opportunity to see how the law impacted "the individual before the Court," the very thing that Griswold praised Brennan for doing so well.

Such an omission is not only atypical of Brennan opinions in general, but it is even atypical of his opinions in the procedural due process area. When, for example, in *Bell v. Burson*, the state took away the driver's license of an uninsured motorist who had had an accident, Brennan was quick to point out in his majority opinion that the motorist was a minister who needed to drive to get around to his congregation. . . .

One might attempt to attribute this omission to an absence of such facts in the record, but not only were these facts available in the record, they were discussed at length by the district court. For example, the district court discussed graphically the plight of Mrs. Angela Velez and her four children who were denied benefits for four months before a post-termination hearing determined the denial to be erroneous:

> [I]n the four months between termination of AFDC [Aid to Families with Dependent Children] benefits and the decision reversing the local agency, Mrs. Velez and her four children, ages one to six, were evicted from her apartment for nonpayment of rent and went to live with her sister, who has nine children and is on relief. Mrs. Velez and three children have been sleeping in two single beds in a small room, and the youngest sleeps in a crib in the same room. Thirteen children and two adults have been living in one apart-

ment, and Mrs. Velez states that she has been unable to feed her children adequately, so that they have lost weight and have been ill.

The district court even added to this account the events that befell another victim of benefit termination, Mrs. Esther Lett. During her time off public assistance, Mrs. Lett and her children had to go to the hospital after having only spoiled chicken and rice to eat, and Mrs. Lett passed out from hunger while waiting in an emergency aid line.

What makes these omissions particularly curious is that Brennan did not just fail to mention these case histories; rather, he came as close as he could to embracing these facts and then failed to use them as support for his decision. In one paragraph, Brennan used three ellipses in quotes of the district court. Each of these omitted a reference to Mrs. Velez or Mrs. Lett. . . .

The questions surrounding Brennan's writing of *Goldberg*, however, are not limited to his treatment of facts. They extend also to his treatment of authority. . . . Although Brennan limited the first sentence of [a] quote to this: "'Against the justified desire to protect public funds must be weighed the individual's overpowering need in this unique situation not to be wrongfully deprived of assistance,'" the district court went on to add "and the startling statistic that post-termination fair hearings apparently override prior decisions to terminate benefits in a substantial number of cases." Thus, Brennan represented the district court's balance as a two factor balancing test when, in fact, it was a three factor test, and the factor Brennan omitted turned out to be the one Brennan would choose not to use.

This is not the only place in *Goldberg* where Brennan took liberties with his authorities. In some places, he used authority inaccurately where he may not have actually needed any authority at all, and he certainly did not need inaccurate ones. It is hard to understand how this use of authority came from the pen of a man whose legal career has been "best character-ized as a triumph of competence."

Although several explanations could be offered for Brennan's uncharacteristic use of law and fact in *Goldberg,* one particularly plausible one is that Brennan felt pressured by [Hugo] Black's dissent in that case. There, Black main-tained that Brennan had no authority for what he was doing in *Goldberg* and was simply letting his conscience be guided by the facts. Such criticism would have hit home with Bren-nan because he felt a certain loyalty to precedent even though he quite willingly acknowledged its limitations. Thus, for Bren-nan the best response to Black's dissent would have been a sterile, factless opinion loaded with authority. Unfortunately, it is hard to write such an opinion and revolutionize an area of the law simultaneously. Quite simply, if the authority existed, one would not need to revolutionize the area of law. Thus, something has to give in that situation, and in this instance, the giving may well be reflected in Brennan's atypical writing of *Goldberg.*

Be that as it may, *Goldberg* did in fact refocus both prop-erty and due process jurisprudence under the Due Process clause, and the significance of that cannot be denied. . . .

Goldberg Interpretation Did Not Last

The years following *Goldberg v. Kelly* may be divided into three periods. In the first, . . . the Court was content to be miles from nowhere. During this period, the Court struggled with a multitude of different approaches to due process, un-able to use any one consistently. In the second period, . . . the Court brought together its most promising due process struc-tures from the first period and set out on the road to find out which would work best. Finally, in the third period, . . . the Court cast the test it had settled upon into the wild world, only to find that a lot of nice things do indeed turn bad out there.

When this ride ended, the *Goldberg* due process test was a shadow of its former self. In particular, though statutory entitlements remained property, the protection property status afforded entitlements fell short of what Brennan had originally envisioned. This should not suggest that *Goldberg* was an empty promise nor that *Goldberg* has little to offer for the future. No one can deny that the world of due process today looks quite different than did the world of due process before *Goldberg*, even if that world is not everything that Brennan might have envisioned. In addition, a number of good ideas presented themselves both in *Goldberg* and in the succeeding cases, and those ideas can still be used to improve the course of clue process analysis. . . .

Is there life for *Goldberg v. Kelly* at twenty-five? Certainly, there remains little reason to cite it. Beyond that, one would hardly retain it as a tribute to Brennan's skill as a legal writer. . . . The opinion, along with the cases that followed it, do little to enhance Justice Brennan's legacy on the Court and his role as one of its most successful leaders. . . .

Goldberg Opinions Still Meaningful

Having acknowledged this much, one can still say not only that there could be life for *Goldberg* at twenty-five but also that we must go back and come to grips with what it tells us about the Constitution and our nation. We are a nation in the midst of a constitutional and structural crisis that has us simultaneously bemoaning our inability to move with a common vision and priding ourselves on splintering into a pluralistic society.

Our problem is not a paradox but simply a puzzle to which *Goldberg* holds the answer. That answer lies in the recognition that both Brennan and Black are right. Our Constitution is both a call to a community that "foster[s] the dignity and well-being of all persons within its borders" by bringing everyone "to participate meaningfully in the life of the community" [Brennan's opinion] and a proclamation of individual autonomy that commands to government, "'thus far and no farther shall you go.'" [Black's opinion]. . .

Black's notion of walls and rights is not unique in American jurisprudence nor is Brennan's notion of community. The two, however, draw upon very different values and structures. Community, at least in one view, proceeds from two recognitions: first, that each has been given her talents not simply for her own autonomous gain but "for the common good" and second, that one does not suffer or celebrate solely as a function of her own status but "[i]f one member suffers, all suffer together with it; if one member is honored, all rejoice together with it." [I Corinthians 12:26] These recognitions would allow Brennan to say that one is injured when her neighbor cannot "participate meaningfully in the life of the community" and that "malaise" is not personal but "societal."

In this view, community is more than bringing "political outgroups to the table and ensur[ing] their effective participation in a dialogue among political equals." More than a call to empathy, community is a call to action, action which would not take place within the traditional political dialogue of power and rights. . . .

Even the images of the two approaches are different. For Brennan's community, the "State" is "We the people." It is Abraham Lincoln's "of the people, by the people, for the people" and [poet] Robert Frost's "salvation in surrender." Ultimately, it allows for President John F. Kennedy's instruction: "Ask not what your country can do for you—ask what you can do for your country." Meanwhile for Black, "State" was an entity inclined toward "unrestrained powers to make life miserable for [its] citizens," a white marble monster posed on the Potomac to strike the little guys.

One might well wonder if these approaches are so different, how they have managed to coexist so long. Willie many answers may explain it, the first is necessity—a necessity bred by two conditions. The first condition is a recognition on the part of the individual that in some areas he cannot submit, or does not want to submit, himself to the majority's will. The second condition is a recognition that the majority will not always respond with compassion toward the individual. When either condition is present, the community model erupts into conflict, and we must resort to identifying rights and building walls to settle the conflict. . . .

Balancing Diversity and Community

One might wonder also how Brennan could be tied to such a comprehensive vision of Constitution as community, when he described the rights established in the Constitution as "a sparkling vision of the supremacy of the human dignity of every individual." Dignity, individuality and self-worth, however, are not exclusively functions of either a community-based or a rights-based social order. Some notions of community emphasize the need of each individual to appreciate and nurture his own personal gifts and to bring them to the community and, consequently, to recognize the necessity of others doing the same. Thus, one could advance that the Constitution protects individuality to guarantee that a diversity of gifts will be brought to the union.

Such a notion would be important for today because twenty-five years after *Goldberg v. Kelly*, the challenge to creating "a more perfect union" is no longer recognizing equality, as perhaps it was after the Civil War, or facilitating assimilation, as it was at the time of *Brown v. Board of Education*. Today, the challenge is dealing with a population that seems intent on asserting its diversity. In *Goldberg*, Brennan gave us a vision of the Constitution that would call that diversity into community, that would rejoice in the meaningful participation of a wide range of gifts shared for the common good. . . .

The challenge facing the nation today is not so different from the one that separated Black and Brennan. Then, as now, it had to be determined how much we want to create opportunities for all "to participate meaningfully in the life of the community" and how much we want to say, "Thus far and no farther shall you go." ...

No matter which road we choose to travel, the road will have its problems. If the Constitution, however, can be seen as defining a relationship among "We the People," then perhaps there is room to be optimistic despite those problems. This is so because for all our failures and frustrations in the area of personal relationships, somehow people continue coming up with new energy, imagination, and resourcefulness to try to make personal relationships work in their lives. The calling is simply to try in the same way to bring new imagination, energy, and resourcefulness to our relationship as a nation. ...

Goldberg, as well as its progeny, still has much to say even after twenty-five years. ...

Perhaps what matters most is not the answer reached but the commitment to finding the right answer. Although the Court ultimately may not have embraced the best test for procedural due process analysis, the justices certainly committed themselves to finding such a test. In hindsight, it is easy to find fault in their inconsistencies, their ideological agendas, and even their writing. Such fault finding, however, shows simply that the members of the Court are mortals subject to human weakness. That should come as no great revelation. More important than such weakness, however, is the commitment that can be found in the hundreds of pages of multiple majority, plurality, concurring, and dissenting opinions that make up this line of cases. Faced with losses like Mrs. Lett's welfare, Mr. Roth's job, and Mr. Stanley's children, the justices repeatedly sought diligently, persistently, and often even passionately for answers that could withstand the test of time, even when it was obvious that the time for a particular answer would not be the present. It is reassuring that the most powerful lawyers in the country can still recognize the importance of the everyday problems affecting the lives of ordinary citizens, even if their solutions are not the ones each of us might select.

CHAPTER 3

Eligibility for Welfare Can Be Conditioned on Consent to Home Visits

Case Overview

Wyman v. James (1971)

Under New York law the Department of Social Services was required to visit the homes of welfare applicants to determine whether they were eligible for Aid to Families with Dependent Children (AFDC) benefits (welfare), and to visit again periodically to see whether there had been any changes in their situation that would affect eligibility. Caseworkers could not enter anyone's home without consent, but people who did not consent lost their welfare benefits.

Barbara James applied for benefits shortly before the birth of her son, Maurice, and did not object to the caseworker's visit. But two years later, when she received a notice that the visit was going to be repeated, she denied permission for it. She phoned the caseworker and said that she was willing to provide any relevant information, but the discussion must not take place at her home. Although told that her welfare payments would be terminated if she did not allow the visit, she declined to give her consent. At a hearing before a review officer, she continued to refuse, and when her benefits were stopped she filed a lawsuit on the grounds that home searches without warrants are prohibited by the Constitution.

The district court ruled in James's favor, holding that a mother receiving AFDC relief could refuse, without forfeiting her right to that relief, the periodic home visit specified by New York's law. It agreed that home visitation is a search and, when neither consented to nor supported by a warrant based on probable cause, it violates the beneficiary's Fourth and Fourteenth Amendment rights. However, a dissenting judge thought it was unrealistic to regard the home visit as a search. He felt that the requirement of a search warrant to be issued only upon a showing of probable cause would make the AFDC program "in effect another criminal statute" and would "introduce a hostile arm's length element into the relationship" between worker and mother, "a relationship which can be effective only when it is based upon mutual confidence and trust." He concluded that the majority's holding struck "a damaging blow" to an important social welfare program.

The U.S. Supreme Court therefore agreed to review the case. While acknowledging that official intrusions into private homes raise concern about Fourth Amendment rights, the Court ruled six to three that home visits by caseworkers are not searches in the sense intended by the Fourth Amendment because their purpose is not to investigate crime and there is no criminal penalty for refusing to allow a visit. Even if the visits did qualify as searches, it said, they would still be constitutional because they are reasonable, and the Fourth Amendment prohibits only unreasonable searches. The majority opinion explained in detail why the justices considered such visitations reasonable.

This ruling set a precedent that has determined the outcome of many other cases, particularly the 2006 case *Sanchez v. County of San Diego*, which the Supreme Court refused to review, thus indicating that it was not willing to overturn *Wyman v. James* as many commentators thought it should. The issue of home visitation is still controversial. It is required in many places, and in some, such as San Diego, it is carried out by law enforcement officers even though the beneficiaries visited are not individually suspected of crime. Some people feel that court sanction of such programs is due to discrimination against the poor. Others believe that it is indeed reasonable to check up on welfare recipients to make sure they are not collecting payments to which they are not entitled.

| *"The caseworker is not a sleuth but rather, we trust, is a friend to one in need."*

Majority Opinion: Home Visitation of Welfare Recipients Is Constitutional

Harry A. Blackmun

Harry A. Blackmun was a justice of the Supreme Court from 1970 to 1994. He is best known as the author of the majority opinion in Roe v. Wade, *the decision that overturned laws restricting abortion. In the following opinion in* Wyman v. James, *he writes that required home visits to welfare recipients are not searches as defined under the Fourth Amendment because they are not criminal investigations and a home cannot be entered without the beneficiary's permission. Furthermore, he says, even if they were classed as searches, they could not be called unreasonable, so the Fourth Amendment would not prohibit them. Such searches serve a valid administrative purpose, he maintains, and the Court has decided that they are not unconstitutional.*

This appeal presents the issue whether a beneficiary of the program for Aid to Families with Dependent Children (AFDC) may refuse a home visit by the caseworker without risking the termination of benefits. . . .

Plaintiff Barbara James is the mother of a son, Maurice, who was born in May 1967. They reside in New York City.

Harry A. Blackmun, majority opinion, *Wyman v. James*, U.S. Supreme Court, January 12, 1971.

Mrs. James first applied for AFDC assistance shortly before Maurice's birth. A caseworker made a visit to her apartment at that time without objection. The assistance was authorized.

Two years later, on May 8, 1969, a caseworker wrote Mrs. James that she would visit her home on May 14. Upon receipt of this advice, Mrs. James telephoned the worker that, although she was willing to supply information 'reasonable and relevant' to her need for public assistance, any discussion was not to take place at her home. The worker told Mrs. James that she was required by law to visit in her home and that refusal to permit the visit would result in the termination of assistance. Permission was still denied.

On May 13 the City Department of Social Services sent Mrs. James a notice of intent to discontinue assistance because of the visitation refusal. The notice advised the beneficiary of her right to a hearing before a review officer. The hearing was requested and was held on May 27. Mrs. James appeared with an attorney at that hearing. They continued to refuse permission for a worker to visit the James home, but again expressed willingness to cooperate and to permit visits elsewhere. The review officer ruled that the refusal was a proper ground for the termination of assistance. His written decision stated:

'The home visit which Mrs. James refuses to permit is for the purpose of determining if there are any changes in her situation that might affect her eligibility to continue to receive Public Assistance, or that might affect the amount of such assistance, and to see if there are any social services which the Department of Social Services can provide to the family.' . . .

Unreasonable Home Searches

When a case involves a home and some type of official intrusion into that home, as this case appears to do, an immediate and natural reaction is one of concern about Fourth Amendment rights and the protection which that Amendment is intended to afford. Its emphasis indeed is upon one of the most precious aspects of personal security in the home: 'The right of the people to be secure in their persons, houses, papers, and effects.' This Court has characterized that right as 'basic to a free society.' And over the years the Court consistently has been most protective of the privacy of the dwelling. In *Camara v. Municipal Court* Mr. Justice [Byron] White, after noting that the 'translation of the abstract prohibition against 'unreasonable searches and seizures' into workable guidelines for the decision of particular cases is a difficult task,' went on to observe, 'Nevertheless, one governing principle, justified by history and by current experience, has consistently been followed: except in certain carefully defined classes of cases, a search of private property without proper consent is 'unreasonable' unless it has been authorized by a valid search warrant.' He pointed out, too, that one's Fourth Amendment protection subsists apart from his being suspected of criminal behavior.

This natural and quite proper protective attitude, however, is not a factor in this case, for the seemingly obvious and simple reason that we are not concerned here with any search by the New York social service agency in the Fourth Amendment meaning of that term. It is true that the governing statute and regulations appear to make mandatory the initial home visit and the subsequent periodic 'contacts' (which may include home visits) for the inception and continuance of aid. It is also true that the caseworker's posture in the home visit is perhaps, in a sense, both rehabilitative and investigative. But this latter aspect, we think, is given too broad a character and far more emphasis than it deserves if it is equated with a search in the traditional criminal law context. We note, too, that the visitation in itself is not forced or compelled, and that the beneficiary's denial of permission is not a criminal act. If consent to the visitation is withheld, no visitation takes place. The aid then never begins or merely ceases, as the case may be. There is no entry of the home and there is no search.

Home Visits Not Unreasonable

If however, we were to assume that a caseworker's home visit, before or subsequent to the beneficiary's initial qualification for benefits, somehow (perhaps because the average beneficiary might feel she is in no position to refuse consent to the visit), and despite its interview nature, does possess some of the characteristics of a search in the traditional sense, we nevertheless conclude that the visit does not fall within the Fourth Amendment's proscription. This is because it does not descend to the level of unreasonableness. It is unreasonableness which is the Fourth Amendment's standard. And Mr. Chief Justice [Earl] Warren observed in *Terry v. Ohio* 'the specific content and incidents of this right must be shaped by the context in which it is as asserted.'

There are a number of factors that compel us to conclude that the home visit proposed for Mrs. James is not unreasonable:

1. The public's interest in this particular segment of the area of assistance to the unfortunate is protection and aid for the dependent child whose family requires such aid for that child. The focus is on the child and, further, it is on the child who is dependent. There is no more worthy object of the public's concern. The dependent child's needs are paramount, and only with hesitancy would we relegate those needs, in the scale of comparative values, to a position secondary to what the mother claims as her rights.

2. The agency, with tax funds provided from federal as well as from state sources, is fulfilling a public trust. The State, working through its qualified welfare agency, has appropriate and paramount interest and concern in seeing and assuring that the intended and proper objects of that tax-produced assistance are the ones who benefit

from the aid it dispenses. Surely it is not unreasonable, in the Fourth Amendment sense or in any other sense of that term, that the State have at its command a gentle means, of limited extent and of practical and considerate application, of achieving that assurance.

3. One who dispenses purely private charity naturally has an interest in and expects to know how his charitable funds are utilized and put to work. The public, when it is the provider, rightly expects the same. It might well expect more, because of the trust aspect of public funds, and the recipient, as well as the caseworker, has not only an interest but an obligation.

4. The emphasis of the New York statutes and regulations is upon the home, upon 'close contact' with the beneficiary, upon restoring the aid recipient 'to a condition of self-support,' and upon the relief of his distress. The federal emphasis is no different. It is upon 'assistance and rehabilitation,' upon maintaining and strengthening family life, and upon 'maximum self-support and personal independence consistent with the maintenance of continuing parental care and protection.' It requires cooperation from the state agency upon specified standards and in specified ways. And it is concerned about any possible exploitation of the child.

5. The home visit, it is true, is not required by federal statute or regulation. But it has been noted that the visit is 'the heart of welfare administration'; that it affords 'a personal, rehabilitative orientation, unlike that of most federal programs'; and that the 'more pronounced service orientation' effected by Congress with the 1956 amendments to the Social Security Act 'gave redoubled importance to the practice of home visiting.' The home visit is an established routine in States besides New York.

6. The means employed by the New York agency are significant. Mrs. James received written notice several days in advance of the intended home visit. The date was specified. Privacy is emphasized. The applicant-recipient is made the primary source of information as to eligibility. Outside informational sources, other than public records, are to be consulted only with the beneficiary's consent. Forcible entry or entry under false pretenses or visitation outside working hours or snooping in the home are forbidden. All this minimizes any 'burden' upon the homeowner's right against unreasonable intrusion.

7. Mrs. James, in fact, on this record presents no specific complaint of any unreasonable intrusion of her home and nothing that supports an inference that the desired home visit had as its purpose the obtaining of information as to criminal activity. She complains of no proposed visitation at an awkward or retirement hour. She suggests no forcible entry. She refers to no snooping. She describes no impolite or reprehensible conduct of any kind. She alleges only, in general and nonspecific terms, that on previous visits and, on information and belief, on visitation at the home of other aid recipients, 'questions concerning personal relationships, beliefs and behavior are raised and pressed which are unnecessary for a determination of continuing eligibility.' Paradoxically, this same complaint could be made of a conference held elsewhere than in the home, and yet this is what is sought by Mrs. James. The same complaint could be made of the census taker's questions. What Mrs. James appears to want from the agency that provides her and her infant son with the necessities for life is the right to receive those necessities upon her own informational terms, to utilize the Fourth Amendment as a wedge for imposing those terms, and to avoid questions of any kind.

8. We are not persuaded, as Mrs. James would have us be, that all information pertinent to the issue of eligibility can be obtained by the agency through an interview at a place other than the home, or, as the District Court majority suggested, by examining a lease or a birth certificate, or by periodic medical examinations, or by interviews with school personnel. Although these secondary sources might be helpful, they would not always assure verification of actual residence or of actual physical presence in the home, which are requisites for AFDC benefits, or of impending medical needs. And, of course, little children, such as Maurice James, are not yet registered in school.

9. The visit is not one by police of uniformed authority, it is made by a caseworker of some training whose primary objective is, or should be, the welfare, not the prosecution, of the aid recipient for whom the worker has profound responsibility. As has already been stressed, the program concerns dependent children and the needy families of those children. It does not deal with crime or with the actual or suspected perpetrators of crime. The caseworker is not a sleuth but rather, we trust, is a friend to one in need.

10. The home visit is not a criminal investigation, does not equate with a criminal investigation, and despite the announced fears of Mrs. James and those who would join her, is not in aid of any criminal proceeding. If the visitation serves to discourage misrepresentation or fraud, such a byproduct of that visit does not impress upon the visit itself a dominant criminal investigative aspect. And if the visit should, by chance, lead to the discovery of fraud and a criminal prosecution should follow, then, even assuming that the evidence discovered upon the home visitation is admissible, an issue upon which we express no opinion, that is a routine

and expected fact of life and a consequence no greater than that which necessarily ensues upon any other discovery by a citizen of criminal conduct.

11. The warrant procedure, which the plaintiff appears to claim to be so precious to her, even if civil in nature, is not without its seriously objectionable features in the welfare context. If a warrant could be obtained (the plaintiff affords us little help as to how it would be obtained), it presumably could be applied for ex parte [by one party], its execution would require no notice, it would justify entry by force, and its hours for execution would not be so limited as those prescribed for home visitation. The warrant necessarily would imply conduct either criminal or out of compliance with an asserted governing standard. Of course, the force behind the warrant argument, welcome to the one asserting it, is the fact that it would have to rest upon probable cause, and probable cause in the welfare context, as Mrs. James concedes, requires more than the mere need of the caseworker to see the child in the home and to have assurance that the child is there and is receiving the benefit of the aid that has been authorized for it. In this setting the warrant argument is out of place.

Refusal Has Consequences

It seems to us that the situation is akin to that where an Internal Revenue Service agent, in making a routine civil audit of a taxpayer's income tax return, asks that the taxpayer produce for the agent's review some proof of a deduction the taxpayer has asserted to his benefit in the computation of his tax. If the taxpayer refuses, there is, absent fraud, only a disallowance of the claimed deduction and a consequent additional tax. The taxpayer is fully within his 'rights' in refusing to produce the proof, but in maintaining and asserting those rights a tax detriment results and it is a detriment of the taxpayer's own making. So here Mrs. James has the 'right' to refuse the home visit, but a consequence in the form of cessation of aid, similar to the taxpayer's resultant additional tax, flows from that refusal. The choice is entirely hers, and nothing of constitutional magnitude is involved. . . .

Mrs. James, is not being prosecuted for her refusal to permit the home visit and is not about to be so prosecuted. Her wishes in that respect are fully honored. We have not been told, and have not found, that her refusal is made a criminal act by any applicable New York or federal statute. The only consequence of her refusal is that the payment of benefits ceases. Important and serious as this is, the situation is no different than if she had exercised a similar negative choice initially and refrained from applying for AFDC benefits. If a statute made her refusal a criminal offense, and if this case were one concerning her prosecution under that statute, *Camara* [*v. Municipal Court*] and *See* [*v. City of Seattle*] would have conceivable pertinency.

Our holding today does not mean, of course, that a termination of benefits upon refusal of a home visit is to be upheld against constitutional challenge under all conceivable circumstances. The early morning mass raid upon homes of welfare recipients is not unknown. But that is not this case. Facts of that kind present another case for another day.

We therefore conclude that the home visitation as structured by the New York statutes and regulations is a reasonable administrative tool; that it serves a valid and proper administrative purpose for the dispensation of the AFDC program; that it is not an unwarranted invasion of personal privacy; and that it violates no right guaranteed by the Fourth Amendment.

> "A restriction of the Fourth Amendment to 'the traditional criminal law context' tramples the ancient concept that a man's home is his castle."

Dissenting Opinion: Fourth Amendment Protection Against Searches Applies to Home Visits

Thurgood Marshall

Thurgood Marshall was the first African American to serve as a justice of the Supreme Court. In the following dissenting opinion in Wyman v. James, *he argues that the Fourth Amendment to the Constitution covers all intrusion into homes by the government, not just those involving suspected crime, and that in any case home visits to welfare recipients do involve investigation that could lead to criminal charges of welfare fraud or child abuse. The Court majority, he says, had no valid grounds for concluding that such searches are not unreasonable and do not require a warrant. In addition, Marshall maintains, regulations of the Department of Health, Education, and Welfare prohibit home visits without the homeowner's consent, and the fact that the only penalty for refusal to consent is loss of welfare benefits does not mean the visits are not coerced. He concludes that the Court has ruled inconsistently with past decisions and the burden of that departure from precedent has been placed on the poor.*

Thurgood Marshall, dissenting opinion, *Wyman v. James*, U.S. Supreme Court, January 12, 1971.

Although I substantially agree with its initial statement of the issue in this case, the Court's opinion goes on to imply that the appellee has refused to provide information germane to a determination of her eligibility for AFDC [Aid to Families with Dependent Children] benefits. The record plainly shows, however, that Mrs. James offered to furnish any information that the appellants desired and to be interviewed at any place other than her home. Appellants rejected her offers and terminated her benefits solely on the ground that she refused to permit a home visit. In addition, appellants make no contention that any sort of probable cause exists to suspect appellee of welfare fraud or child abuse.

Simply stated, the issue in this case is whether a state welfare agency can require all recipients of AFDC benefits to submit to warrantless 'visitations' of their homes. In answering that question, the majority dodges between constitutional issues to reach a result clearly inconsistent with the decisions of this Court. We are told that there is no search involved in this case; that even if there were a search, it would not be unreasonable; and that even if this were an unreasonable search, a welfare recipient waives her right to object by accepting benefits. I emphatically disagree with all three conclusions. Furthermore, I believe that binding regulations of the Department of Health, Education, and Welfare [HEW] prohibit appellants from requiring the home visit.

Home Visits Involve a Search

The Court's assertion that this case concerns no search 'in the Fourth Amendment meaning of that term' is neither 'obvious' nor 'simple.' I should have thought that the Fourth Amendment governs all intrusions by agents of the public upon personal security. As Mr. Justice [John Marshall] Harlan has said: '(T)he Constitution protects the privacy of the home against all unreasonable intrusion of whatever character. "(It applies) to all invasions on the part of the government and its employees of the sanctity of a man's home."'

This Court has rejected as 'anomalous' the contention that only suspected criminals are protected by the Fourth Amendment. In an era of rapidly burgeoning governmental activities and their concomitant inspectors, caseworkers, and researchers, a restriction of the Fourth Amendment to 'the traditional criminal law context' tramples the ancient concept that a man's home is his castle. Only last Term, we reaffirmed that this concept has lost none of its vitality.

Even if the Fourth Amendment does not apply to each and every governmental entry into the home, the welfare visit is not some sort of purely benevolent inspection. No one questions the motives of the dedicated welfare caseworker. Of course, caseworkers seek to be friends, but the point is that they are also required to be sleuths. The majority concedes that the 'visitation' is partially investigative, but claims that this investigative aspect has been given too much emphasis. Emphasis has indeed been given. Time and again, in briefs and at oral argument, appellants emphasized the need to enter AFDC homes to guard against welfare fraud and child abuse, both of which are felonies. The New York statutes provide emphasis by requiring all caseworkers to report any evidence of fraud that a home visit uncovers. And appellants have strenuously emphasized the importance of the visit to provide evidence leading to civil forfeitures including elimination of benefits and loss of child custody.

Actually, the home visit is precisely the type of inspection proscribed by *Camara v. Municipal Court* and its companion case, *See v. City of Seattle*, except that the welfare visit is a more severe intrusion upon privacy and family dignity. Both the home visit and the searches in those cases may convey benefits to the householder. Fire inspectors give frequent advice concerning fire prevention, wiring capacity, and other matters, and obvious self-interest causes many to welcome the fire or safety inspection. Similarly, the welfare caseworker may provide welcome advice on home management and child care. Nonetheless, both searches may result in the imposition of civil penalties—loss or reduction of welfare benefits or an order to upgrade a housing defect. The fact that one purpose of the visit is to provide evidence that may lead to an elimination of benefits is sufficient to grant appellee protection since *Camara* stated that the Fourth Amendment applies to inspections which can result in only civil violations. But here the case is stronger since the home visit, like many housing inspections, may lead to criminal convictions.

The Court attempts to distinguish *See* and *Camara* by telling us that those cases involved 'true' and 'genuine' searches. The only concrete distinction offered is that *See* and *Camara* concerned criminal prosecutions for refusal to permit the search. The *Camara* opinion did observe that one could be prosecuted for a refusal to allow that search; but, apart from the issue of consent, there is neither logic in, nor precedent for, the view that the ambit of the Fourth Amendment depends not on the character of the governmental intrusion but on the size of the club that the State wields against a resisting citizen. Even if the magnitude of the penalty were relevant, which sanction for resisting the search is more severe? For protecting the privacy of her home, Mrs. James lost the sole means of support for herself and her infant son. For protecting the privacy of his commercial warehouse, Mr. See received a $100 suspended fine.

Most Warrantless Searches Unreasonable

Conceding for the sake of argument that someone might view the 'visitation' as a search, the majority nonetheless concludes that such a search is not unreasonable. However, its mode of reaching that conclusion departs from the entire history of Fourth Amendment case law. Of course, the Fourth Amendment test is reasonableness, but in determining whether a search is reasonable, this Court is not free merely to balance, in a totally ad hoc fashion, any number of subjective factors. An unbroken line of cases holds that, subject to a few narrowly drawn exceptions, any search without a warrant is constitutionally unreasonable. In this case, no suggestion that evidence will disappear, that a criminal will escape, or that an officer will be injured, justifies the failure to obtain a warrant. Instead, the majority asserts what amounts to three state interests that allegedly render this search reasonable. None of these interests is sufficient to carve out a new exception to the warrant requirement.

First, it is argued that the home visit is justified to protect dependent children from 'abuse' and 'exploitation.' These are heinous crimes, but they are not confined to indigent households. Would the majority sanction, in the absence of probable cause, compulsory visits to all American homes for the purpose of discovering child abuse? Or is this Court prepared to hold as a matter of constitutional law that a mother, merely because she is poor, is substantially more likely to injure or exploit her children? Such a categorical approach to an entire class of citizens would be dangerously at odds with the tenets of our democracy.

Second, the Court contends that caseworkers must enter the homes of AFDC beneficiaries to determine eligibility. Interestingly, federal regulations do not require the home visit. In fact, the regulations specify the recipient himself as the primary source of eligibility information thereby rendering an inspection of the home only one of several alternative secondary sources. The majority's implication that a biannual home visit somehow assures the verification of actual residence or actual physical presence in the home strains credulity in the context of urban poverty. Despite the caseworker's responsibility for dependent children, he is not even required to see the children as a part of the home visit. Appellants offer scant explanation for their refusal even to attempt to utilize public records, expenditure receipts, documents such as leases, non-home interviews, personal financial records, sworn declarations, etc. all sources that governmental agencies regularly accept as adequate to establish eligibility for other public benefits. In this setting, it ill behooves appellants to refuse to utilize informational sources less drastic than an invasion of the privacy of the home.

We are told that the plight of Mrs. James is no different from that of a taxpayer who is required to document his right to a tax deduction, but this analogy is seriously flawed. The record shows that Mrs. James has offered to be interviewed anywhere other than her home, to answer any questions, and to provide any documentation that the welfare agency desires. The agency curtly refused all these offers and insisted on its 'right' to pry into appellee's home. Tax exemptions are also governmental 'bounty.' A true analogy would be an Internal Revenue Service requirement that in order to claim a dependency exemption, a taxpayer must allow a specially trained IRS agent to invade the home for the purpose of questioning the occupants and looking for evidence that the exemption is being properly utilized for the benefit of the dependent. If such a system were even proposed, the cries of constitutional outrage would be unanimous.

Appellants offer a third state interest that the Court seems to accept as partial justification for this search. We are told that the visit is designed to rehabilitate, to provide aid. This is strange doctrine indeed. A paternalistic notion that a complaining citizen's constitutional rights can be violated so long as the State is somehow helping him is alien to our Nation's philosophy. More than 40 years ago, Mr. Justice [Louis] Brandeis warned: 'Experience should teach us to be most on our guard to protect liberty when the Government's purposes are beneficent' [*Olmstead v. United States*].

Throughout its opinion, the majority alternates between two views of the State's interest in requiring the home visit.

First we are told that the State's purpose is benevolent so that no search is involved. Next we are told that the State's need to prevent child abuse and to avoid the misappropriation of welfare funds justifies dispensing with the warrant requirement. But when all the State's purposes are considered at one time, I can only conclude that the home visit is a search and that, absent a warrant, that search is unreasonable.

Although the Court does not agree with my conclusion that the home visit is an unreasonable search, its opinion suggests that even if the visit were unreasonable, appellee has somehow waived her right to object. Surely the majority cannot believe that valid Fourth Amendment consent can be given under the threat of the loss of one's sole means of support. Nor has Mrs. James waived her rights. Had the Court squarely faced the question of whether the State can condition welfare payments on the waiver of clear constitutional rights, the answer would be plain. The decisions of this Court do not support the notion that a State can use welfare benefits as a wedge to coerce 'waiver' of Fourth Amendment rights. . . . This Court last Term reaffirmed *Sherbert* [*v. Verner*] and *Speiser* [*v. Randall*] as applicable to the law of public welfare: 'Relevant constitutional restraints apply as much to the withdrawal of public assistance benefits as to disqualification for unemployment compensation . . . denial of a tax exemption . . . or . . . discharge from public employment' [*Goldberg v. Kelly*].

Unconsented Home Visits Prohibited

The Court's examination of the constitutional issues presented by this case has constrained me to respond. It would not have been necessary to reach these questions for I believe that HEW regulations, binding on the States, prohibit the unconsented home visit.

The federal Handbook of Public Assistance Administration provides: 'The (state welfare) agency especially guards against violations of legal rights and common decencies in such areas as entering a home by force, or without permission, or under false pretenses; making home visits outside of working hours, and particularly making such visits during sleeping hours.'

Although the tone of this language is descriptive, HEW requirements are stated in terms of principles and objectives; and appellants do not contend that this regulation is merely advisory. Instead, appellants respond with the tired assertion that consent obtained by threatening termination of benefits constitutes valid permission under this regulation. There is no reason to suspect that HEW shares this crabbed view of consent. The Handbook itself insists on careful scrutiny of purported consent. Section 2200(a) is designed to protect the privacy of welfare recipients, and it would be somewhat ironic to adopt a construction of the regulation that provided that any person who invokes his privacy rights ceases to be a recipient.

Appellants next object that the home visit has long been a part of welfare administration and has never been disapproved by HEW. The short answer to this is that we deal with only the unconsented home visit. The general utility and acceptance of the home visit casts little light on whether HEW might prefer not to impose the visit on unwilling recipients. Appellants also remind us that the Federal Government itself requires a limited number of home visits for sampling purposes. However, while there may well be a special need to employ mandatory visits as a part of quality control samples, Mrs. James' home was not a part of such a sample. . . .

In deciding that the homes of AFDC recipients are not entitled to protection from warrantless searches by welfare caseworkers, the Court declines to follow prior case law and employs a rationale that, if applied to the claims of all citizens, would threaten the vitality of the Fourth Amendment. This Court has occasionally pushed beyond established constitutional contours to protect the vulnerable and to further basic human values. I find no little irony in the fact that the burden of today's departure from principled adjudication is placed upon the lowly poor. Perhaps the majority has explained why a commercial warehouse deserves more protection than does this poor woman's home. I am not convinced; and, therefore, I must respectfully dissent.

> *"Because we are bound by* Wyman, *we conclude that . . . home visits do not qualify as searches within the meaning of the Fourth Amendment."*

Wyman v. James Settled the Issue of Visiting Welfare Recipients' Homes

A. Wallace Tashima

A. Wallace Tashima is a judge of the U.S. Court of Appeals, Ninth Circuit. In the following opinion in Sanchez v. County of San Diego, *a 2006 case challenging mandatory home visits to welfare recipients in San Diego, he rules that the Supreme Court decision in* Wyman v. James *is binding despite the differences between the two cases. Furthermore, he says, later Supreme Court holdings have provided additional grounds for concluding that the San Diego home visit program is permissible under the Constitution.*

In 1997, the San Diego County District Attorney ("D.A.") initiated a program whereby all San Diego County residents who submit welfare applications under California's welfare program ("CalWORKS"), and are not suspected of fraud or ineligibility, are automatically enrolled in Project 100%. The parties are essentially in agreement as to the structure and operation of Project 100%. Under Project 100%, all applicants receive a home visit from an investigator employed by the D.A.'s office. The visit includes a "walk through" to gather eli-

A. Wallace Tashima, court's opinion, *Sanchez v. County of San Diego*, U.S. Court of Appeals, Ninth Circuit, September 19, 2006.

gibility information that is then turned over to eligibility technicians who compare that information with information supplied by the applicant. Specifically, the investigator views items confirming that: (1) the applicant has the amount of assets claimed; (2) the applicant has an eligible dependent child; (3) the applicant lives in California; and (4) an "absent" parent does not live in the residence.

When applicants submit an application for welfare benefits, they are informed that they will be subject to a mandatory home visit in order to verify their eligibility. Applicants are also informed that the home visit must be completed prior to aid being granted, but are not given notice of the exact date and time the visit will occur. The visits are generally made within 10 days of receipt of the application and during regular business hours, unless a different time is required to accommodate an applicant's schedule. The home visits are conducted by investigators from the Public Assistance Fraud Division of the D.A.'s office, who are sworn peace officers with badges and photo identification. The investigators wear plain clothes and do not carry weapons.

The actual home visit consists of two parts: an interview with the applicant regarding information submitted during the intake process, and a "walk through" of the home. The visit takes anywhere from 15 minutes to an hour, with five to 10 minutes generally allocated to the "walk through." If the applicant refuses to allow a home visit, the investigator immediately terminates the visit and reports that the applicant failed to cooperate. This generally results in the denial of benefits. The denial of welfare aid is the only consequence of refusing to allow the home visit; no criminal or other sanctions are imposed for refusing consent.

The "walk through" portion of the home visit is also conducted with the applicant's consent. The applicant is asked to lead the "walk through" and the investigator is trained to look for items in plain view. The investigator will also ask the applicant to view the interior of closets and cabinets, but will only do so with the applicant's express permission. While the investigators are required to report evidence of potential criminal wrongdoing for further investigation and prosecution, there is no evidence that any criminal prosecutions for welfare fraud have stemmed from inconsistencies uncovered during a Project 100% home visit. . . .

The Fourth Amendment to the United States Constitution protects the "right of the people to be secure in their persons, houses, papers, and effects, against unreasonable searches and seizures." Appellants argue that the warrantless home visits conducted under Project 100% violate the Fourth Amendment's protection against unreasonable searches as it applies to the State of California via the Fourteenth Amendment.

Home Visits Are Not Searches

We must first decide the threshold question of whether the home visits quality as searches within the meaning of the Fourth Amendment. Appellants contend that the home visits are searches because they are highly intrusive and their purpose is to discover evidence of welfare fraud. The Supreme Court, however, has held that home visits for welfare verification purposes are not searches under the Fourth Amendment. *See Wyman v. James.*

In *Wyman*, the Court held that home visits by a social worker, made pursuant to the administration of New York's welfare program, were not searches because they were made for the purpose of verifying eligibility for benefits, and not as part of a criminal investigation. . . . Importantly, the visits were not conducted as part of a *criminal* investigation. Accordingly, the Court concluded that the visits did not rise to the level of a "search in the traditional criminal law context."

Wyman directly controls the instant [present] case. Here, as in *Wyman*, all prospective welfare beneficiaries are subject to mandatory home visits for the purpose of verifying eligibility, and not as part of a criminal investigation. The investigators conduct an in-home interview and "walk through," looking for inconsistencies between the prospective beneficiary's application and her actual living conditions. As in *Wyman*, the home visits are conducted with the applicant's consent, and if consent is denied, the visit will not occur. Also as in *Wyman*, there is no penalty for refusing to consent to the home visit, other than denial of benefits. The fact that the D.A. investigators who make the Project 100% home visits are sworn peace officers does not cause the home visits to rise to the level of a "search in the traditional criminal law context" because the visits' underlying purpose remains the determination of welfare eligibility.

Therefore, because we are bound by *Wyman*, we conclude that the Project 100% home visits do not qualify as searches within the meaning of the Fourth Amendment. . . .

Home Searches Are Reasonable

The district court found that the Project 100% home visits, even if considered searches, were reasonable under *Wyman*. Although we need not reach the question to decide Appellants' Fourth Amendment challenge, because the home visits do not constitute searches under *Wyman*, we agree with the district court that even if the home visits are searches under the Fourth Amendment, they are reasonable.

In *Wyman*, the Court concluded that the home visits, even if considered a search, were valid under the Fourth Amendment "because [they] did not descend to the level of unreasonableness . . . which is the Fourth Amendment's standard." The Court weighed several factors in balancing the governmental interest in conducting home visits against the intrusion into the welfare applicant's privacy. . . .

Here, as in *Wyman*, the home visits serve the important governmental interests of verifying an applicant's eligibility for welfare benefits and preventing fraud. As the Court acknowledged in *Wyman*, the public has a strong interest in ensuring that aid provided from tax dollars reaches its proper and intended recipients. While the visits in this case differ from those in *Wyman* in that they are conducted by peace officers, this distinction does not transform a Project 100% visit into a "search in the traditional criminal law context." . . .

The Project 100% home visits also have many of the same procedural safeguards that the *Wyman* Court found significant. Applicants are given notice that they will be subject to a mandatory home visit and visits generally occur only during normal business hours. When the investigators arrive to conduct the visit, they must ask for consent to enter the home. If the applicant does not consent to the visit, or withdraws consent at anytime during the visit, the visit will not begin or will immediately be terminated, as the case may be.

Finally, the Court's concern that a warrant requirement would pose serious administrative difficulties in the welfare context is also present in this case. As the Court in *Wyman* explained, "if a warrant could be obtained, it presumably could be applied for *ex parte* [by one party], its execution would require no notice, it would justify entry by force, and its hours for execution would not be so limited as those prescribed for home visitation." This type of warrant requirement would make home visits more intrusive than the County's current suspicionless home visit program because welfare applicants' rights and privacy would be subject to greater infringement.

Therefore, because the Project 100% visits serve an important governmental interest, are not criminal investigations, occur with advance notice and the applicant's consent, and alleviate the serious administrative difficulties associated with welfare eligibility verification, we hold that the home visits are reasonable under the Supreme Court's decision in *Wyman*.

"Special Needs" Cases

While *Wyman* provides adequate, independent grounds for holding that the Project 100% home visits are reasonable, the Supreme Court's Fourth Amendment jurisprudence has evolved significantly since *Wyman*, providing further support for this conclusion. Subsequent to *Wyman*, the Court articulated its "special needs" exception to the warrant requirement, holding that "[a] search unsupported by probable cause can be constitutional ... when special needs, beyond the normal need for law enforcement, make the warrant and probable-cause requirement impracticable" [*Griffin v. Wisconsin*]. ...

In *Griffin*, the Supreme Court examined whether the State's operation of its probation system was a "special need" that justified the warrantless search of a probationer's home, based on reasonable grounds to suspect the presence of contraband. The Court held that the operation of a probation system was a valid "special need," explaining that the system worked towards genuine rehabilitation through intensive supervision and that a "warrant requirement would interfere to an appreciable degree." ...

In *Ferguson v. City of Charleston*, however, the Court held that a public hospital's policy of identifying and testing mothers whose children tested positive for drugs at birth was not justified under the "special needs" doctrine because "the immediate objective of the searches was to generate evidence *for law enforcement purposes.*" ... The Court explained that the "central and indispensable feature of the policy from its inception was the use of law enforcement to coerce the patients into substance abuse treatment," and concluded that "the purpose actually served by the searches is ultimately indistinguishable from the general interest in crime control."

Ferguson turned on the fact that the searches at issue were conducted for general law enforcement purposes. The Court emphasized that while the drug testing program partially served a non-criminal purpose, the program's efficacy was ultimately tied to the successful prosecution of mothers whose children tested positive for drugs. In *Wyman*, however, the Court specifically noted that home visits in the welfare context primarily serve the administrative function of eligibility verification, which is not a general law enforcement purpose. As discussed *supra*, [above] the primary purpose of the Project 100% home visits is to verify eligibility for welfare benefits. While there may be a fine line between verifying eligibility and investigating fraud, the record here supports that the visits are indeed used primarily for verification and prevention purposes. . . .

Reasonable in Light of "Special Need"

Because we conclude that the administration of the County's welfare system presents a "special need" beyond those of normal law enforcement, we must now determine whether this need is "important enough to override the individual's acknowledged privacy interest [and] sufficiently vital to suppress the Fourth Amendment's normal requirement of individualized suspicion." Specifically, we consider: (1) the nature of the privacy interest upon which the search intrudes; (2) the character of the intrusion; and (3) the important of the government interest at stake.

Here, the nature of Appellants' privacy interest is significant because the government is conducting searches of their homes, a traditionally protected area of personal privacy. As illustrated by *Griffin*, however, a person's relationship with the state can reduce that person's expectation of privacy even within the sanctity of the home. When eligibility depends, in part, upon a person's physical residence in the state and actual presence at the place designated as their residence, verification of eligibility may be reasonably required in the form of the home visit under review here in order to ensure that funds are properly spent. Moreover, the home visits are conducted with the applicant's express consent, thus, further reducing the applicant's expectation of privacy. Therefore, it is reasonable for welfare applicants who desire direct cash governmental aid to undergo eligibility verification through home visits.

Next, we must weigh the character of the intrusion on Appellants' privacy. Appellants argue that the home visits are virtually unlimited in scope. As discussed above, however, the record demonstrates that the procedures used in conducting the home visits are designed to reduce the intrusion on the applicant's privacy. Investigators only examine areas of the home that they believe will provide relevant information pertaining to the applicant's welfare eligibility. If at any point before or during the visit, the applicant refuses to consent, or withdraws consent, the visit ends immediately. Additionally, inspections are completed in a reasonable amount of time and there is no evidence that any of the applicants has been subjected to abusive behavior during the home visits.

Finally, we must analyze the need for the intrusion in light of its efficacy in achieving the governmental interests at stake. Appellants argue that there is no statistically significant evidence that Project 100% has actually reduced welfare fraud. The County, however, produced data showing that, during the five-year period during which Project 100% was implemented, the overall denial rate increased from 40.6% to 47.7%, and there was an additional 4–5% increase in application withdrawals. While it is difficult to measure the precise efficacy of Project 100%, these empirical observations support the logical connection between the home visits and their intended purpose. Moreover, the visits are an effective method of verifying eligibility for benefits, and, at a minimum, the visits provide an important deterrent effect.

Appellants also contend that all necessary information for purposes of verification can be obtained from other sources and that the home visits merely duplicate the intake interviews. The Supreme Court has stressed, however, that the Fourth Amendment does not require that the government use the least intrusive means "because the logic of such elaborate less-restrictive alternative arguments could raise insuperable barriers to the exercise of virtually all search-and-seizure powers." [*Pottawatomie v.*] *Earls*. More importantly, the Court has already rejected a similar argument in *Wyman*, explaining that "[a]lthough . . . secondary sources might be helpful, they would not always assure verification of actual residence or of actual physical presence in the home, which are requisites for AFDC [Aid to Families with Dependent Children] benefits. . . ."

Accordingly, because the Project 100% home visits are conducted in a reasonable manner, and serve an important administrative purpose, the Supreme Court's "special needs" line of cases provides further support for our conclusion that the home visits are reasonable under the Fourth Amendment.

"We would not sanction such an intrusion as a condition of any other public benefit, save welfare. This is a shameful jurisprudence."

Wyman v. James and Later Decisions Based on It Should Be Overturned

Steven D. Schwinn

Steven D. Schwinn is an associate professor of law at the John Marshall Law School in Chicago. In the following viewpoint he argues that the Supreme Court ruling in Wyman v. James *has proved to be a durable barrier against the claim that mandatory home visits to welfare recipients are unconstitutional searches under the Fourth Amendment, since later courts have held to the standards set by that case. In his opinion, the* Wyman v. James *decision was mistaken because the Court did not consider the coercive nature of such visits or the question of whether they were sufficiently related to the government's purpose. He says that it ought to be overturned; until it is, however, attorneys should not base future cases on the Fourth Amendment, but should instead argue that the visits have no essential relationship to the goals of the welfare program and therefore cannot be justified.*

In 1971 the U.S. Supreme Court ruled in *Wyman v. James* that the U.S. Constitution did not protect welfare recipients from mandatory home visits by the government as a condition of receiving public assistance. That case has proved to be

Steven D. Schwinn, "Reconstructing the Constitutional Case Against Mandatory Welfare Home Visits," *Clearinghouse Review: Journal of Poverty Law and Policy*, May/June 2008, pp. 42–47. Reproduced by permission.

a durable barrier against the claim that welfare home visits run afoul of the Fourth Amendment's protection against unreasonable searches—that mandatory home visits are an unconstitutional condition on receiving welfare.

The claim is based on the unconstitutional-conditions doctrine, which holds that the government may not condition benefits upon the surrender of individual constitutional rights. The doctrine applies to any government benefit and any constitutional right, although it applies differently to different benefits and to different rights. But even as the doctrine has evolved into various (and sometimes confused) principles in other areas, the unconstitutional-conditions doctrine under the Fourth Amendment has remained consistently and exclusively bound to the restrictive holding in *James*.

Thus thirty-five years after *James* came down, the Ninth Circuit upheld San Diego's mandatory welfare home visits in an opinion remarkably similar to *James* itself. The case reaffirmed *James*'s supremacy in challenges to welfare home visits under the unconstitutional-conditions doctrine, suggesting (if there were any doubt) that plaintiffs need to find a new theory. . . .

Inadequacies of *Wyman v. James*

In *James* the Supreme Court upheld New York's mandatory and warrantless home visits for all Aid to Families with Dependent Children applicants and recipients against a Fourth Amendment challenge. The visits in that case were primarily rehabilitative, with emphasis on "restoring the aid recipient 'to a condition of self-support,' and upon the relief of his distress." To that end, the visits were conducted by "a caseworker of some training"—not a police officer or an investigator—"whose primary objective is, or should be, the welfare, not the prosecution, of the aid recipient." Moreover, applicants and recipients received written notice, including a specified date for the visit, several days before the visit.

The *James* Court's holdings are familiar. First, the Court held that the visits were primarily rehabilitative and therefore not Fourth Amendment "searches" at all. The Court distinguished New York's welfare home visits from "true search[es] for violations" that might result in criminal prosecution and to which the Fourth Amendment warrant requirement applied. Second, the Court ruled out of hand that the visits were fully consensual; it did not even seriously address the inherently coercive nature of mandatory home visits for a welfare applicant or recipient. And consensual visits implicated no Fourth Amendment interests. And, third, the Court held that even if the visits were Fourth Amendment "searches," they were fully reasonable. The Court fleetingly reviewed the characteristics of the visits and the interests at stake—purporting to balance eleven distinct "factors" related to the visits and to the parties' interests—and concluded that the Fourth Amendment would demand no warrant, even if the visits were "searches." Absent from the Court's balancing was any meaningful scrutiny of the relationship between the home visit program and the goals that the government sought to achieve.

James set the standards for all future Fourth Amendment challenges of mandatory welfare home visits—and it set them high. In the wake of *James*, only investigative visits, and not those that are rehabilitative in nature, are "searches" under the Fourth Amendment. Moreover, only visits involving some uncommon measure of coercion are nonconsensual and thus trigger a Fourth Amendment reasonableness inquiry. And, even if a visit raised Fourth Amendment concerns, only those "unreasonable" warrantless searches—as measured by the eleven factors in *James*—run afoul of the Fourth Amendment.

Standard Used in *Sanchez v. San Diego*

These standards were most recently on full display in *Sanchez v. San Diego*. In *Sanchez* the Ninth Circuit upheld San Diego's mandatory welfare home visit and home walk-through program, "Project 100%," against a Fourth Amendment challenge. The Ninth Circuit's analysis precisely mirrored that of the Supreme Court in *James*. But, unlike New York's home visit program upheld in *James*, Project 100% subjected applicants to a visit by an investigator and sworn peace officer from the Public Assistance Fraud Division of the district attorney's office. Project 100% investigators are trained to verify welfare eligibility and to investigate welfare fraud, not to assess a family's needs or to recommend assistance. In fact, as the dissent noted, investigators are specifically trained *not to* counsel applicants since the exclusive purpose of the program is preventing fraud and legal compliance. Investigators are trained to look for items in plain view and to ask to see the interiors of closets, cabinets, and the like; investigators have a duty to report perceived evidence of any unlawful activity, whether related to welfare eligibility or not. Applicants are not given notice of the date and time of the visit, although visits usually occur within ten days of the application.

Just as the Supreme Court ruled in *James*, the Ninth Circuit ruled that the Project 100% visits were not Fourth Amendment searches; that in any event they were consensual; and that, even if they were searches, they were reasonable under the *James* factors. On this last point—and just like the Supreme Court in *James*—the Ninth Circuit gave scant attention to any relationship or fit between the Project 100% visits and the goals of the welfare program, instead focusing on balancing the plaintiff's interest in privacy against the government's various interests in conducting the visits.

In short, the Ninth Circuit's ruling in *Sanchez* suggests that the only bounds on mandatory welfare visits under *James* are those found to apply to the wholly arbitrary and extreme welfare raids that marked a particularly embarrassing and indecent chapter in the history of public benefits. Thus, if *Sanchez* suggests how far the *James* principles extend, *Sanchez* also illustrates the inadequacy of the *James* approach in challenging clearly investigatory searches under the Fourth Amendment and the unconstitutional-conditions doctrine.

Sanchez tells us (yet again) that all but the most intrusive investigatory visits are not Fourth Amendment searches; that nearly any visit as a condition of welfare is consensual; and that even if a welfare visit program constitutes a Fourth Amendment search, the government's interests will nearly always outweigh the plaintiff's. We would not sanction such an intrusion as a condition of any other public benefit, save welfare. This is a shameful jurisprudence, and *James* and its progeny ought to be overruled. Until they are, however, we need a new approach.

An Alternative Approach

One of the more notable developments in the unconstitutional-conditions doctrine in the last twenty-five years is the advent of the essential-nexus test in *Nollan v. California Coastal Commission.* The Nollans sought to demolish their beach-front house and to build a larger home on their property. The local zoning commission granted a building permit, but the commission conditioned the permit on the Nollans providing an easement to allow the public to pass across a portion of their private beach property between two public beaches. The Nollans sued, claiming that the condition violated the Fifth Amendment takings clause.

The Supreme Court agreed. It ruled that the condition was not sufficiently related to the proposed construction—that there was no essential nexus [connection] between the easement and the proposed new home—and that the condition was therefore invalid. . . .

The Court thus concludes that a government condition insufficiently related to its broader end is invalid, whether or not the underlying government action would be constitutional if performed directly. Stated only slightly differently: a government action performed indirectly is valid only if sufficiently related to the government purpose in acting directly; this apparently holds irrespective of the constitutionality of the government's direct act. Or yet differently: the greater power to deny benefits includes the lesser power to condition benefits only if an essential nexus links the condition and the purpose pose in denying benefits entirely.

The Court reaffirmed this remarkable principle in *Dolan v. City of Tigard* and went a step further in clarifying it. . . .

If *Nollan* and *Dolan* apply beyond the Fifth Amendment—as apparently by their own terms they do—they offer a powerful opportunity to reframe and recalibrate unconstitutional-conditions arguments.

The essential-nexus test offers both considerable and unrealized benefits in unconstitutional-conditions challenges to mandatory welfare home visits. As an initial matter, the threshold essential-nexus test turns the traditional Fourth Amendment arguments on their head: rather than arguing first that home visits are Fourth Amendment searches and that they are coerced (and only secondarily that the visits are "unreasonable"), plaintiffs raising the essential-nexus test may argue first that the visits fail to harmonize with the goals of the welfare program. This move sidesteps the nearly hopeless but threshold arguments under *James* (and now *Sanchez*) that home visits are Fourth Amendment searches and that they are coerced; instead the move redirects the inquiry to the relationship between the condition and the goals of the welfare program. . . .

This approach would offer new opportunities to introduce evidence and present arguments on the fitness between home visits and welfare program goals. For example, the plaintiff's evidence and arguments in *Sanchez* relating to the effectiveness of Project 100%—including any evidence of actual welfare fraud, perhaps even in comparison to fraud in other government programs—would become immediately relevant to show whether Project 100% serves the goals of the broader welfare program under an essential-nexus approach, even as the court in *Sanchez* all but ignored that evidence in considering the plaintiff's Fourth Amendment challenge under *James*. Similarly the plaintiff's argument that no other local government in California used fraud investigators from a district attorney's office translates directly into fitness arguments under an essential-nexus approach, even as the court could dismiss this argument under *James*. These are but two examples based on the actual evidence in *Sanchez*. We can only imagine how the record may have developed differently with a focus on the essential-nexus test instead of the Fourth Amendment and *James*.

The essential-nexus approach does not require abandoning the Fourth Amendment and *James*. Plaintiffs may still argue alternatively that home visits violate the Fourth Amendment. Indeed they must: only by thus pressing *James* will we ever lay it to rest.

"The state has repeatedly exempted the poor from the full measure of privacy protections at the core of our constitutional identity."

Wyman v. James Deprived the Poor of the Constitutional Protections Given to Others

Jordan C. Budd

Jordan C. Budd is a professor of law at Franklin Pierce Law Center in New Hampshire and the former legal director of the American Civil Liberties Union Foundation of San Diego and Imperial Counties in Southern California. He represented the plaintiff class in Sanchez v. San Diego, *a case for which the court's opinion is included in this chapter of the present volume. In the following viewpoint he states that there has long been discrimination against the poor in situations involving the right to privacy and that this trend is accelerating. Welfare recipients not under suspicion of wrongdoing are often required to submit to intrusive visits to their homes, and the courts have sanctioned this practice. Budd argues that this is because of a long-standing view of the poor as morally inferior. The Supreme Court's opinion in* Wyman v. James *reads like a parental lecture, he says, and has led to bias by later courts in judging violations of the Fourth Amendment.*

Jordan C. Budd, "A Fourth Amendment for the Poor Alone: Subconstitutional Status and the Myth of the Inviolate Home," *Indiana Law Journal*, vol. 85, Spring 2010. Reproduced by permission.

For much of our nation's history, the poor have faced pervasive discrimination in the exercise of fundamental rights. Nowhere has the impairment been more severe than in the area of privacy. Acting with the acquiescence of a complicit judiciary, the state has repeatedly exempted the poor from the full measure of privacy protections at the core of our constitutional identity—most often through the imposition of highly intrusive conditions upon government's provision of subsistence aid or its recognition of the custodial interests of indigent parents. . . .

Far from a matter of receding historical interest, the diminution of the poor's fourth Amendment right to domestic privacy has accelerated in recent years and now represents a powerful theme within the jurisprudence of poverty. Triggering this development has been a series of legal challenges to increasingly aggressive administrative practices adopted by various localities in the wake of federal welfare-reform legislation. As a precondition to the provision of public assistance, some jurisdictions now require that applicants submit to an unannounced and suspicionless search of their homes by law-enforcement investigators seeking evidence of welfare fraud—a practice that pushes far beyond the verification requirements previously imposed on aid applicants. In turning back challenges to these privacy intrusions, courts have significantly curtailed the protections of the Fourth Amendment as applied to the poor.

While the courts that sanction these practices disclaim any sort of poverty-based classification underlying their analysis, this Article argues that no other rationale withstands scrutiny. Neither precedent nor the principled extension of existing Fourth Amendment doctrine justifies recent outcomes or explains why those holdings should not be applied to authorize a vast—and, thus, unacceptable—expansion of suspicionless search practices directed at the homes of the less destitute. The developing jurisprudence thus represents an implicit concession that the poor constitute a subconstitutional class for purposes of the Fourth Amendment, and a confirmation that judicial bias continues to powerfully burden indigent litigants. Framed most charitably, the decisions understand poverty as a condition of moral culpability and thus accept it as a surrogate for the individualized suspicion of wrongdoing that otherwise would be required to justify the intrusions at issue. The premise of the guilty poor, tracing back centuries, remains very much alive and well in contemporary American law. . . .

As government subsidies, grants, and financial aid to other groups and individuals proliferated during the twentieth century, the longstanding premise that the poor sacrificed their right of privacy in exchange for public assistance stood increasingly in tension with the undiminished rights of others receiving government largesse. Inevitably, the continuing use of home visits, late-night raids, and related surveillance techniques through the 1950s and 1960s collided with the Fourth Amendment as activists in the nascent welfare-rights movement sought to extend increasingly robust protections against warrantless home searches to welfare recipients. In *Wyman v. James*, the Supreme Court addressed the question and confirmed that the rhetoric of domestic sanctity stopped at the doorstep of the poor.

Resolving the Conflict in Favor of the State

The Supreme Court's 1971 decision in *Wyman* considered whether public officials could condition welfare benefits upon the requirement that recipients consent to periodic home visits by caseworkers. In endorsing the requirement, the Court began its discussion by acknowledging the home's special status in Fourth Amendment jurisprudence:

> When a case involves a home and some type of official intrusion into that home, as this case appears to do, an immediate and natural reaction is one of concern about Fourth Amendment rights and the protection which that Amend-

ment is intended to afford. Its emphasis indeed is upon one of the most precious aspects of personal security in the home. . . . And over the years the Court consistently has been most protective of the privacy of the dwelling.

Having acknowledged "[t]his natural and quite proper protective attitude," the Court immediately declared that it was irrelevant to the case—"for the seemingly obvious and simple reason that we are not concerned here with any search . . . in the Fourth Amendment meaning of that term." In a cursory passage, the Court asserted that home visits fell outside the scope of the Fourth Amendment because of the predominantly rehabilitative (as opposed to investigative) purpose of the caseworker's visit and the fact that a visit, if any, occurred only by consent. These rationales attracted considerable criticism. First, the Court itself had previously defined a Fourth Amendment search in far more inclusive terms that captured virtually any intrusion by state agents upon personal privacy—a standard that surely reached the entry at issue in *Wyman*. Second, the Court's focus on the rehabilitative purpose of the visit conflicted with settled precedent establishing that the objective of the state's intrusion, and the civil or criminal consequences (if any) that follow, are irrelevant to the initial determination of whether the entry falls within the ambit of Fourth Amendment scrutiny. Finally, the Court's discussion of consent made no sense: free and voluntary consent serves to validate—not eliminate—a Fourth Amendment search.

As an alternative ground, the Court held that the visit, even if construed as a search under the Fourth Amendment, was reasonable and thus permissible based on the balance of relevant interests. Since the visit at issue involved neither a warrant nor any individualized suspicion of wrongdoing, the Court's ruling in this respect withheld from welfare recipients virtually all of the procedural and substantive protections available under the Fourth Amendment. In support of its conclusion, the Court recited an "ad hoc" array of reasonableness factors that variously ignored or misconstrued precedent, trivialized the intrusive and often adversarial nature of the caseworker's presence within the home, and stigmatized poor parents based on archaic stereotypes.

The Court's reasonableness analysis placed significant emphasis on the fact that no criminal sanctions attended the refusal to authorize a home visit—instead, aid simply ceased. The Court asserted that this consideration distinguished the case from earlier and more protective decisions involving civil searches, such as *Camara v. Municipal Court* and *See v. City of Seattle*, in which, criminal sanctions might result from the refusal to permit an administrative home inspection. The argument, however, turned those decisions on their head. The entire thrust of *Camara* and *See* was to discard the civil-criminal distinction for purposes of assessing the applicability of the Fourth Amendment warrant requirement and to overrule prior authority—specifically, *Franks v. Maryland*—to the contrary. . . .

Idealizing the Role of the Caseworker

Another factor heavily relied upon by the *Wyman* Court was the caseworker's purportedly trusting and supportive relationship with the recipient and the unobtrusive nature of the home entry itself. Evoking the mythic "friendly visitor" of the nineteenth century, the Court declared that the caseworker was not an adversarial "sleuth but rather, we trust, a friend to one in need." The decision repeatedly returned to the "rehabilitative" and "personal" nature of the visit, coupled with the absence of "forcible entry or entry under false pretenses or visitation outside working hours or snooping in the home," and on that basis asserted that the intrusive dimension of the search was trivial. This analysis notably omitted two central considerations: first, that the "friend[ly]" visit was an involuntary entry into the home of the aid recipient—the paramount zone of privacy that, in other contexts, the Court had repeatedly acknowledged to be sacrosanct; and, second, that the presence of a caseworker was inherently intrusive and disruptive of the family's autonomy, irrespective of the absence of any "impolite or reprehensible conduct." ... Notably, the Court's effort in this regard to depict the visits as "personal" and "rehabilitative" conspicuously ignored that the caseworker was required to initiate a criminal investigation if anything observed within the home raised suspicions of fraud.

Completing the Court's reasonableness analysis was a factor squarely at odds with the preceding proposition. In emphasizing the state's "paramount" interest in entering the home, the Court shifted away from the conception of a gentle and helpful caseworker to the need for investigative scrutiny of the residence to assure the protection of the children within. Here the Court turned its attention to adult recipients and rendered a depiction of them in the long tradition of the morally-bereft poor. Indigent children, we are told, require protection from "possible exploitation" at the hands of their avaricious parents, who otherwise might divert aid to satisfy their own desires. . . .

To corroborate this asserted need for investigative scrutiny, the Court turned to Mrs. James herself—despite the fact that the case involved a challenge to the defendant's general search practices, which operated without suspicion of or regard for the plaintiff's particular conduct—and suggested that she was precisely the kind of abusive and immoral parent who demonstrated the need to intrude upon the homes of the poor. "We have examined Mrs. James' case record," the Court solemnly intoned [in a footnote], and

> [i]t is revealing as to [her] failure ever really to satisfy the requirements of eligibility; as to constant and repeated demands; as to attitude toward the caseworker; as to reluctance to cooperate; and as to evasiveness; and as to occasional

belligerency. There are indications that all was not always well with the infant Maurice. . . . The picture is a sad and unhappy one.

The Court's premise of the immoral poor, now corroborated and embodied by an anecdotal caricature of Mrs. James herself, supplied the state with the necessary interest to exempt all indigent parents from otherwise applicable constitutional protections. . . . By imputing to impoverished parents this universal risk of misconduct, *Wyman* implicitly transformed the suspicionless home searches at issue into the sort of cause-based investigative entries traditionally associated with the protections of the Fourth Amendment. Supplanting the need for individualized suspicion, the recurring premise of the immoral poor opened the doors of Mrs. James' home for the protection of her child. . . .

Much of the opinion reads less like constitutional adjudication than a parental lecture: a benevolent patriarch imposes upon a wayward child "a gentle means, of limited extent and of practical and considerate application," to assure that she properly spends her allowance. The implicit message is that the poor stand apart for purposes of rights enforcement. By virtue of their moral infirmity, coupled with their indebtedness to the state for its support, the indigent approach the Court not as litigants but as supplicants in hopes of dispensation. Thus the task is not to determine constitutional entitlement but rather to judge a plea for indulgence, which the *Wyman* Court deemed unworthy.

Contemporary Application of *Wyman*

As an affirmation of longstanding bias and an implicit declaration that the poor are simply different for purposes of constitutional analysis, *Wyman* challenged the lower courts to define its reach. Should the ruling herald a new era of retrenchment in the poor's quest for equal justice, or should it instead be cast as an outlier—a decision so poorly reasoned and at odds with allied precedent that its holding must be limited to the narrowest plausible construction?

In the 1970s and 1980s, a handful of lower courts embraced the latter view. Asserting that the *Wyman* Court "emphasized the peculiar factual situation of the case" and noting the inconsistency of its reasoning with other Fourth Amendment precedents, the D.C. Circuit concluded in 1975 that the Supreme Court had "limited *Wyman* to its particular factual context." In 1979, a district court declined to apply *Wyman* to search practices utilized by a mobile unit of caseworkers who visited the homes of recipients accused of welfare fraud. The court noted that "[t]he majority opinion in *Wyman v. James* is not without conceptual problems, and, in view of the vigorous, persuasive three-judge dissenting opinions, the holding must be restricted to the boundaries imposed by the facts to avoid glaring inconsistency with prior search and seizure cases." Another district court echoed the conclusion in a 1988 decision declining to extend *Wyman* to on-site observations of home-schooled students. Noting that the inspections under review were "analogous" to several key features of the *Wyman* visits, the court nonetheless concluded that *Wyman* "seems inconsistent with prevailing fourth amendment analysis, and the precedential effect of *Wyman* probably should be limited to the specific facts of that case."

Other courts, while not expressing doubt regarding the force of the precedent, have declined to extend it in related areas. The topic most frequently addressed in this context has been the permissibility of warrantless search practices in child abuse and neglect investigations. Despite the relationship of *Wyman* and its rationale to the challenged policies, most federal courts have declined to uphold the searches—most often because of the potential criminal implications of an abuse finding. As one district court explained, "[t]o accept the defendants' claims about the reach of *Wyman* would give the state unfettered and absolute authority to enter private homes and disrupt the tranquility of family life on nothing more than an anonymous rumor that something might be amiss." The consensus, however, is not universal. A district court in Illinois, for example, relied on *Wyman* to conclude that a warrantless strip search of suspected abuse victims neither implicated the Fourth Amendment nor was unreasonable in the absence of probable cause.

Judicial reluctance to extend the reach of *Wyman* has only gone so far—and, not surprisingly, is least evident when the targets of intrusion are exclusively poor. Accordingly, within the classic context of welfare administration, the courts have shown little restraint in embracing and enlarging the precedent. In considering challenges to new and highly intrusive administrative practices arising out of the welfare-reform movement of the 1980s and 1990s, lower courts have not merely conformed to *Wyman*'s analysis but aggressively extended its reasoning beyond the scope of the original ruling—consigning aid applicants to unannounced and exhaustive searches of their bedrooms, bathrooms, drawers, and closets by law enforcement officers looking exclusively for evidence of ineligibility or fraud. In sanctioning these extraordinarily invasive practices in the absence of a warrant or suspicion of wrongdoing, the courts have abandoned any credible pretense of addressing the Fourth Amendment rights of the poor on shared terms with others.

CHAPTER 4

Welfare Recipients Who Move to Another State Are Entitled to Its Benefits

Case Overview

Saenz v. Roe (1999)

During the last decades of the twentieth century the federal government and the governments of many states took steps to reform the welfare system, which was costing taxpayers more and more and was sometimes abused by people who succeeded in collecting payments they were not entitled to and did not really need. The extent to which such abuse occurred, and the measures adopted to curb it, were extremely controversial.

In 1992 the state of California enacted a law limiting new residents' welfare payments to the amount they would have received in their former state of residence. Many citizens viewed this as a reasonable way of saving the state money and of ensuring that people did not move there just to collect its generous welfare benefits. Others considered it unfair, arguing that there was no reason why newcomers should get less than long-term residents and that because the cost of living in California was higher than in most other states, welfare recipients could not survive on payments that were adequate elsewhere.

Three women, all of whom had come to California to escape abusive family situations, filed suit against the state in opposition to the new law. The welfare payments to which the law entitled them were much lower than California's normal grants and made no allowance for their increased cost of living. The district court issued a temporary restraining order preventing the law from going into effect, the court of appeals upheld that order, and the U.S. Supreme Court agreed to consider the case. However, it did not do so, as the law was invalidated for technical legal reasons and remained inoperative until a new welfare law, the Personal Responsibility and Work Opportunity Reconciliation Act of 1996 (PRWORA) was passed by the U.S. Congress.

PRWORA replaced the old welfare system, Aid to Families with Dependent Children (AFDC), with Temporary Assistance to Needy Families (TANF). TANF expressly authorized states to give welfare recipients who had been in the state less than a year only as much as they would have received in the state they came from, even if they had been in the other state only a short time. So another suit was filed, again opposing California's law but also challenging the constitutionality of its authorization by PRWORA. Again a restraining order was issued by the lower courts, and in 1998 the case finally reached the Supreme Court.

In a previous case, *Shapiro v. Thompson* (1969), the Court had decided that denying welfare payments to new residents was an impermissible restriction on citizens' right to travel and that it was unconstitutional under the equal protection clause of the Fourteenth Amendment. In *Saenz v. Roe*, California argued that its law was not enacted for the purpose of discouraging needy persons from moving there and that it did not affect the right to travel because new residents were not ineligible for welfare; they simply received lesser amounts than established residents. The Court, ruling seven to two, held that this argument was irrelevant because the right to travel includes the right of new residents to receive treatment equal to that of other residents. It also stated that there was no danger of people moving to California just long enough to collect welfare benefits, since unlike a subsidized college education or a divorce, such benefits could not be enjoyed after leaving the state.

Although the state's desire to save money was a legitimate aim, the Court said, there was no justification for achieving that aim by discriminatory means. And PRWORA's authorization of the law did not change this, since Congress cannot authorize states to violate the Fourteenth Amendment.

> *"Permissible justifications for discrimination between residents and nonresidents are simply inapplicable to a nonresident's exercise of the right to move into another State and become a resident of that State."*

Majority Opinion: The Fourteenth Amendment Guarantees the Right to Travel

John Paul Stevens

Until his retirement in 2010, John Paul Stevens was the oldest and longest-serving member of the Supreme Court and was generally considered to be the leader of its liberal faction. In the following majority opinion in Saenz v. Roe, he points out that the privileges and immunities clause of the Fourteenth Amendment to the Constitution bars discrimination between residents and nonresidents of a state without a substantial reason. There is no danger that people will move to a state just to collect its welfare benefits, he says, since those benefits are used only while within the state, unlike a subsidized college education or a divorce, for which length of residence requirements are justifiable. He declares that it is unconstitutional to limit the welfare payments of new residents to what they would have received in their former states because neither their length of residence nor where they came from has any bearing on their need for benefits. The mere fact that limiting welfare benefits would save the state money is

John Paul Stevens, majority opinion, *Saenz v. Roe*, U.S. Supreme Court, May 17, 1999.

not an appropriate rationale, Stevens declares; such reasoning would also allow states to deny new residents other residential benefits such as schools, parks, and even police and fire protection.

California is not only one of the largest, most populated, and most beautiful States in the Nation; it is also one of the most generous. Like all other States, California has participated in several welfare programs authorized by the Social Security Act and partially funded by the Federal Government. Its programs, however, provide a higher level of benefits and serve more needy citizens than those of most other States. . . .

In 1992, in order to make a relatively modest reduction in its vast welfare budget, the California Legislature enacted section 11450.03 of the state Welfare and Institutions Code. That section sought to change the California AFDC [Aid to Families with Dependent Children] program by limiting new residents, for the first year they live in California, to the benefits they would have received in the State of their prior residence. . . .

On December 21, 1992, three California residents who were eligible for AFDC benefits filed an action [*Green v. Anderson*] in the Eastern District of California challenging the constitutionality of the durational residency requirement in [the new law]. Each plaintiff alleged that she had recently moved to California to live with relatives in order to escape abusive family circumstances. . . .

The District Court issued a temporary restraining order and, after a hearing, preliminarily enjoined implementation of the statute. District Judge [David] Levi found that the statute "produces substantial disparities in benefit levels and makes no accommodation for the different costs of living that exist in different states." . . . He concluded that the statute placed "a penalty on the decision of new residents to migrate to the State and be treated on an equal basis with existing residents."

In his view, if the purpose of the measure was to deter migration by poor people into the State, it would be unconstitutional for that reason. And even if the purpose was only to conserve limited funds, the State had failed to explain why the entire burden of the saving should be imposed on new residents. The Court of Appeals summarily affirmed for the reasons stated by the District Judge. . . .

Accordingly, [the measure] remained inoperative until after Congress enacted the Personal Responsibility and Work Opportunity Reconciliation Act of 1996 (PRWORA).

PRWORA replaced the AFDC program with TANF [Temporary Assistance for Needy Families]. The new statute expressly authorizes any State that receives a block grant under TANF to "apply to a family the rules (including benefit amounts) of the [TANF] program . . . of another State if the family has moved to the State from the other State and has resided in the State for less than 12 months." . . .

Even if members of an eligible family had lived in California all of their lives, but left the State "on January 29th, intending to reside in another state, and returned on April 15th," their benefits are determined by the law of their State of residence from January 29 to April 15, assuming that that level was lower than California's. Moreover, the lower level of benefits applies regardless of whether the family was on welfare in the State of prior residence and regardless of the family's motive for moving to California. . . .

The Lower Courts' Decision

On April 1, 1997, the two respondents filed this action in the Eastern District of California making essentially the same claims asserted by the plaintiffs in *Anderson v. Green* but also challenging the constitutionality of PRWORA's approval of the durational residency requirement. . . . Judge Levi concluded that the existence of the federal statute did not affect the legal analysis in his prior opinion in *Green*.

He did, however, make certain additional comments on the parties' factual contentions. He noted that the State did not challenge plaintiffs' evidence indicating that, although California benefit levels were the sixth highest in the Nation in absolute terms, when housing costs are factored in, they rank 18th; that new residents coming from 43 States would face higher costs of living in California; and that welfare benefit levels actually have little, if any, impact on the residential choices made by poor people. On the other hand, he noted that the availability of other programs such as homeless assistance and an additional food stamp allowance of $1 in stamps for every $3 in reduced welfare benefits partially offset the disparity between the benefits for new and old residents. Notwithstanding those ameliorating facts, the State did not disagree with plaintiffs' contention that [the law] would create significant disparities between newcomers and welfare recipients who have resided in the State for over one year.

The State relied squarely on the undisputed fact that the statute would save some $10.9 million in annual welfare costs—an amount that is surely significant even though only a relatively small part of its annual expenditures of approximately $2.9 billion for the entire program. It contended that this cost saving was an appropriate exercise of budgetary authority as long as the residency requirement did not penalize the right to travel. The State reasoned that the payment of the same benefits that would have been received in the State of prior residency eliminated any potentially punitive aspects of the measure. Judge Levi concluded, however, that the relevant comparison was not between new residents of California and the residents of their former States, but rather between the new residents and longer term residents of California. He therefore again enjoined the implementation of the statute.

Without finally deciding the merits, the Court of Appeals affirmed his issuance of a preliminary injunction. . . .

The Right to Travel

The word "travel" is not found in the text of the Constitution. Yet the "constitutional right to travel from one State to another" is firmly embedded in our jurisprudence [*United States v. Guest*]. Indeed, as Justice [Potter] Stewart reminded us in *Shapiro v. Thompson*, the right is so important that it is "assertable against private interference as well as governmental action . . . a virtually unconditional personal right, guaranteed by the Constitution to us all."

In *Shapiro*, we reviewed the constitutionality of three statutory provisions that denied welfare assistance to residents of Connecticut, the District of Columbia, and Pennsylvania, who had resided within those respective jurisdictions less than one year immediately preceding their applications for assistance. Without pausing to identify the specific source of the right, we began by noting that the Court had long "recognized that the nature of our Federal Union and our constitutional concepts of personal liberty unite to require that all citizens be free to travel throughout the length and breadth of our land uninhibited by statutes, rules, or regulations which unreasonably burden or restrict this movement." We squarely held that it was "constitutionally impermissible" for a State to enact durational residency requirements for the purpose of inhibiting the migration by needy persons into the State. We further held that a classification that had the effect of imposing a penalty on the exercise of the right to travel violated the Equal Protection Clause "unless shown to be necessary to promote a compelling governmental interest," and that no such showing had been made.

In this case California argues that [the new law] was not enacted for the impermissible purpose of inhibiting migration by needy persons and that, unlike the legislation reviewed in *Shapiro*, it does not penalize the right to travel because new arrivals are not ineligible for benefits during their first year of residence. . . .

The "right to travel" discussed in our cases embraces at least three different components. It protects the right of a citizen of one State to enter and to leave another State, the right to be treated as a welcome visitor rather than an unfriendly alien when temporarily present in the second State, and, for those travelers who elect to become permanent residents, the right to be treated like other citizens of that State.

It was the right to go from one place to another, including the right to cross state borders while en route, that was vindicated in *Edwards v. California*. . . . The right of "free ingress and regress to and from" neighboring States, which was expressly mentioned in the text of the Articles of Confederation, may simply have been "conceived from the beginning to be a necessary concomitant of the stronger Union the Constitution created."

The second component of the right to travel is, however, expressly protected by the text of the Constitution. The first sentence of Article IV, section 2, provides: "The Citizens of each State shall be entitled to all Privileges and Immunities of Citizens in the several States."

Thus, by virtue of a person's state citizenship, a citizen of one State who travels in other States, intending to return home at the end of his journey, is entitled to enjoy the "Privileges and Immunities of Citizens in the several States" that he visits. . . . The Clause "does bar discrimination against citizens of other States where there is no substantial reason for the discrimination beyond the mere fact that they are citizens of other States." There may be a substantial reason for requiring the nonresident to pay more than the resident for a hunting license, or to enroll in the state university, but our cases have not identified any acceptable reason for qualifying the protection afforded by the Clause for "the 'citizen of State A who ventures into State B' to settle there and establish a home" [*Zobel v. Williams*]. Permissible justifications for discrimination between residents and nonresidents are simply inapplicable to a nonresident's exercise of the right to move into another State and become a resident of that State.

Rights of Newly Arrived Citizens

What is at issue in this case, then, is this third aspect of the right to travel—the right of the newly arrived citizen to the same privileges and immunities enjoyed by other citizens of the same State. That right is protected not only by the new arrival's status as a state citizen, but also by her status as a citizen of the United States. That additional source of protection is plainly identified in the opening words of the Fourteenth Amendment:

> All persons born or naturalized in the United States, and subject to the jurisdiction thereof, are citizens of the United States and of the State wherein they reside. No State shall make or enforce any law which shall abridge the privileges or immunities of citizens of the United States. . . .

Despite fundamentally differing views concerning the coverage of the Privileges or Immunities Clause of the Fourteenth Amendment, . . . it has always been common ground that this Clause protects the third component of the right to travel. Writing for the majority in the *Slaughter-House Cases*, Justice [Samuel] Miller explained that one of the privileges conferred by this Clause "is that a citizen of the United States can, of his own volition, become a citizen of any State of the Union by a *bonâ fide* residence therein, with the same rights as other citizens of that State." Justice [Joseph] Bradley, in dissent, used even stronger language to make the same point:

> The states have not now, if they ever had, any power to restrict their citizenship to any classes or persons. A citizen of the United States has a perfect constitutional right to go to and reside in any State he chooses, and to claim citizenship therein, and an equality of rights with every other citizen; and the whole power of the nation is pledged to sustain him

in that right. He is not bound to cringe to any superior, or to pray for any act of grace, as a means of enjoying all the rights and privileges enjoyed by other citizens. . . .

Because this case involves discrimination against citizens who have completed their interstate travel, the State's argument that its welfare scheme affects the right to travel only "incidentally" is beside the point. Were we concerned solely with actual deterrence to migration, we might be persuaded that a partial withholding of benefits constitutes a lesser incursion on the right to travel than an outright denial of all benefits. But since the right to travel embraces the citizen's right to be treated equally in her new State of residence, the discriminatory classification is itself a penalty.

It is undisputed that respondents and the members of the class that they represent are citizens of California and that their need for welfare benefits is unrelated to the length of time that they have resided in California. We thus have no occasion to consider what weight might be given to a citizen's length of residence if the bona fides of her claim to state citizenship were questioned. Moreover, because whatever benefits they receive will be consumed while they remain in California, there is no danger that recognition of their claim will encourage citizens of other States to establish residency for just long enough to acquire some readily portable benefit, such as a divorce or a college education, that will be enjoyed after they return to their original domicile. . . .

Thus, within the broad category of citizens who resided in California for less than a year, there are many who are treated like lifetime residents. And within the broad sub-category of new arrivals who are treated less favorably, there are many smaller classes whose benefit levels are determined by the law of the States from whence they came. To justify [the law], California must therefore explain not only why it is sound fiscal policy to discriminate against those who have been citizens for less than a year, but also why it is permissible to apply such a variety of rules within that class. . . .

Fallacy of the State's Arguments

Disavowing any desire to fence out the indigent, California has instead advanced an entirely fiscal justification for its multitiered scheme. The enforcement of [the measure] will save the State approximately $10.9 million a year. The question is not whether such saving is a legitimate purpose but whether the State may accomplish that end by the discriminatory means it has chosen. An evenhanded, across-the-board reduction of about 72 cents per month for every beneficiary would produce the same result. But our negative answer to the question does not rest on the weakness of the State's purported fiscal justification. It rests on the fact that the Citizenship Clause of the Fourteenth Amendment expressly equates citizenship with residence. . . . Neither the duration of respondents' California residence, nor the identity of their prior States of residence, has any relevance to their need for benefits. Nor do those factors bear any relationship to the State's interest in making an equitable allocation of the funds to be distributed among its needy citizens. As in *Shapiro*, we reject any contributory rationale for the denial of benefits to new residents:

> But we need not rest on the particular facts of these cases. Appellants' reasoning would logically permit the State to bar new residents from schools, parks, and libraries or deprive them of police and fire protection. Indeed it would permit the State to apportion all benefits and services according to the past tax contributions of its citizens.

In short, the State's legitimate interest in saving money provides no justification for its decision to discriminate among equally eligible citizens.

The question that remains is whether congressional approval of durational residency requirements in the 1996 amendment to the Social Security Act somehow resuscitates the constitutionality of [the measure]. That question is readily answered, for we have consistently held that Congress may not authorize the States to violate the Fourteenth Amendment. Moreover, the protection afforded to the citizen by the Citizenship Clause of that Amendment is a limitation on the powers of the National Government as well as the States. . . .

The Solicitor General suggests that the State's discrimination might be acceptable if California had limited the disfavored subcategories of new citizens to those who had received aid in their prior State of residence at any time within the year before their arrival in California. The suggestion is ironic for at least three reasons: It would impose the most severe burdens on the neediest members of the disfavored classes; it would significantly reduce the savings that the State would obtain, thus making the State's claimed justification even less tenable; and, it would confine the effect of the statute to what the Solicitor General correctly characterizes as "the invidious purpose of discouraging poor people generally from settling in the State."

Citizens of the United States, whether rich or poor, have the right to choose to be citizens "of the State wherein they reside" [U.S. Constitution, Fourteenth Amendment, Section one]. The States, however, do not have any right to select their citizens. The Fourteenth Amendment, like the Constitution itself, was, as Justice [Benjamin] Cardozo put it, "framed upon the theory that the peoples of the several states must sink or swim together, and that in the long run prosperity and salvation are in union and not division."

"If States can require individuals to reside in-state for a year before exercising the right to educational benefits [or] the right to terminate a marriage, . . . then States may surely do the same for welfare benefits."

Dissenting Opinion: It Is Reasonable for a State to Require Evidence of Permanent Residence

William Rehnquist

William Rehnquist became a justice of the U.S. Supreme Court in 1972, and in 1986 he became chief justice, a position he held until his death in 2005. He was a strong conservative who believed in a strict interpretation of the Constitution. In the following dissenting opinion in Saenz v. Roe, *he argues that the right to travel and the right to become a citizen of another state are separate, and that the former is irrelevant to the case. The Court's decision, he says, ignores the need to determine whether newcomers are actually residents who intend to stay before providing them with the benefits available to established residents. In his opinion, since residence requirements have been judged constitutional for eligibility for in-state college tuition rates, getting a divorce, or voting in primary elections, the same should be true of welfare benefits.*

William Rehnquist, dissenting opinion, *Saenz v. Roe*, U.S. Supreme Court, May 17, 1999.

The Court today breathes new life into the previously dormant Privileges or Immunities Clause of the Fourteenth Amendment—a Clause relied upon by this Court in only one other decision, *Colgate v. Harvey*, overruled five years later by *Madden v. Kentucky*. It uses this Clause to strike down what I believe is a reasonable measure falling under the head of a "good-faith residency requirement." Because I do not think any provision of the Constitution—and surely not a provision relied upon for only the second time since its enactment 130 years ago—requires this result, I dissent.

The Right to Travel

Much of the Court's opinion is unremarkable and sound. The right to travel clearly embraces the right to go from one place to another, and prohibits States from impeding the free interstate passage of citizens. The state law in *Edwards v. California*, (1941), which prohibited the transport of any indigent person into California, was a classic barrier to travel or migration and the Court rightly struck it down. . . .

I also have no difficulty with aligning the right to travel with the protections afforded by the Privileges and Immunities Clause of Article IV, Section 2, to nonresidents who enter other States "intending to return home at the end of [their] journey." Nonresident visitors of other States should not be subject to discrimination solely because they live out of State. Like the traditional right-to-travel guarantees discussed above, however, this Clause has no application here, because respondents expressed a desire to stay in California and become citizens of that State. Respondents therefore plainly fall outside the protections of Article IV, Section 2.

Finally, I agree with the proposition that a "citizen of the United States can, of his own volition, become a citizen of any State of the Union by a *bonâ fide* residence therein, with the same rights as other citizens of that State" [*Slaughter-House Cases*].

But I cannot see how the right to become a citizen of another State is a necessary "component" of the right to travel, or why the Court tries to marry these separate and distinct rights. A person is no longer "traveling" in any sense of the word when he finishes his journey to a State which he plans to make his home. Indeed, under the Court's logic, the protections of the Privileges or Immunities Clause recognized in this case come into play only when an individual *stops* traveling with the intent to remain and become a citizen of a new State. The right to travel and the right to become a citizen are distinct, their relationship is not reciprocal, and one is not a "component" of the other. . . .

The Court today tries to clear much of the underbrush created by these prior right-to-travel cases, abandoning its effort to define what residence requirements deprive individuals of "important rights and benefits" or "penalize" the right to travel. Under its new analytical framework, a State, outside certain ill-defined circumstances, cannot classify its citizens by the length of their residence in the State without offending the Privileges or Immunities Clause of the Fourteenth Amendment. The Court thus departs from *Shapiro* [*v. Thompson*] and its progeny, and, while paying lipservice to the right to travel, the Court does little to explain how the right to travel is involved at all. Instead, as the Court's analysis clearly demonstrates, this case is only about respondents' right to immediately enjoy all the privileges of being a California citizen in relation to that State's ability to test the good-faith assertion of this right. . . .

Need for Residence Requirements

In unearthing from its tomb the right to become a state citizen and to be treated equally in the new State of residence, however, the Court ignores a State's need to assure that only persons who establish a bona fide residence receive the benefits provided to current residents of the State. The *Slaughter-*

House dicta [nonbinding statements] at the core of the Court's analysis specifically conditions a United States citizen's right to "become a citizen of any state of the Union" and to enjoy the "same rights as other citizens of that State" on the establishment of a "*bona fide residence therein.*" Even when redefining the right to travel in *Shapiro* and its progeny, the Court has "always carefully distinguished between bona fide residence requirements, which seek to differentiate between residents and nonresidents, and residence requirements, such as durational, fixed date, and fixed point residence requirements, which treat established residents differently based on the time they migrated into the State" [*Attorney General of New York v.*] *Soto-Lopez.*

Thus, the Court has consistently recognized that while new citizens must have the same opportunity to enjoy the privileges of being a citizen of a State, the States retain the ability to use bona fide residence requirements to ferret out those who intend to take the privileges and run. . . .

While the physical presence element of a bona fide residence is easy to police, the subjective intent element is not. It is simply unworkable and futile to require States to inquire into each new resident's subjective intent to remain. Hence, States employ objective criteria such as durational residence requirements to test a new resident's resolve to remain before these new citizens can enjoy certain in-state benefits. Recognizing the practical appeal of such criteria, this Court has repeatedly sanctioned the State's use of durational residence requirements before new residents receive in-state tuition rates at state universities. The Court has declared: "The State can establish such reasonable criteria for in-state status as to make virtually certain that students who are not, in fact, *bona fide* residents of the State, but have come there solely for educational purposes, cannot take advantage of the in-state rates" [*Vlandis v. Kline*] (1973). The Court has done the same in upholding a 1-year residence requirement for eligibility to obtain a divorce in state courts, and in upholding political party registration restrictions that amounted to a durational residency requirement for voting in primary elections.

If States can require individuals to reside in-state for a year before exercising the right to educational benefits, the right to terminate a marriage, or the right to vote in primary elections that all other state citizens enjoy, then States may surely do the same for welfare benefits. Indeed, there is no material difference between a 1-year residence requirement applied to the level of welfare benefits given out by a State, and the same requirement applied to the level of tuition subsidies at a state university. The welfare payment here and in-state tuition rates are cash subsidies provided to a limited class of people, and California's standard of living and higher education system make both subsidies quite attractive. Durational residence requirements were upheld when used to regulate the provision of higher education subsidies, and the same deference should be given in the case of welfare payments.

False Distinction Between Various Benefits

The Court today recognizes that States retain the ability to determine the bona fides of an individual's claim to residence, but then tries to avoid the issue. It asserts that because respondents' need for welfare benefits is unrelated to the length of time they have resided in California, it has "no occasion to consider what weight might be given to a citizen's length of residence if the bona fides of her claim to state citizenship were questioned." But I do not understand how the absence of a link between need and length of residency bears on the State's ability to objectively test respondents' resolve to stay in California. There is no link between the need for an education or for a divorce and the length of residence, and yet States may use length of residence as an objective yardstick to channel their benefits to those whose intent to stay is legitimate.

In one respect, the State has a greater need to require a durational residence for welfare benefits than for college eligibility. The impact of a large number of new residents who immediately seek welfare payments will have a far greater impact on a State's operating budget than the impact of new residents seeking to attend a state university. In the case of the welfare recipients, a modest durational residence requirement to allow for the completion of an annual legislative budget cycle gives the State time to decide how to finance the increased obligations.

The Court tries to distinguish education and divorce benefits by contending that the welfare payment here will be consumed in California, while a college education or a divorce produces benefits that are "portable" and can be enjoyed after individuals return to their original domicile. But this "you can't take it with you" distinction is more apparent than real, and offers little guidance to lower courts who must apply this rationale in the future. Welfare payments are a form of insurance, giving impoverished individuals and their families the means to meet the demands of daily life while they receive the necessary training, education, and time to look for a job. The cash itself will no doubt be spent in California, but the benefits from receiving this income and having the opportunity to become employed or employable will stick with the welfare recipient if they stay in California or go back to their true domicile. Similarly, tuition subsidies are "consumed" in-state but the recipient takes the benefits of a college education with him wherever he goes. A welfare subsidy is thus as much an investment in human capital as is a tuition subsidy, and their attendant benefits are just as "portable." ...

I therefore believe that the durational residence requirement challenged here is a permissible exercise of the State's power to "assur[e] that services provided for its residents are enjoyed only by residents" *Martinez* [*v. Bynum*]. The 1-year period established in [the new law] is the same period this

Court approved in *Starns* [*v. Malkerson*] and [*Sosna v. Iowa*]. The requirement does not deprive welfare recipients of all benefits; indeed, the limitation has no effect whatsoever on a recipient's ability to enjoy the full 5-year period of welfare eligibility; to enjoy the full range of employment, training, and accompanying supportive services; or to take full advantage of health care benefits under Medicaid. This waiting period does not preclude new residents from all cash payments, but merely limits them to what they received in their prior State of residence. Moreover, as the Court recognizes, any pinch resulting from this limitation during the 1-year period is mitigated by other programs such as homeless assistance and an increase in food stamp allowance. The 1-year period thus permissibly balances the new resident's needs for subsistence with the State's need to ensure the bona fides of their claim to residence.

Finally, Congress' express approval of durational residence requirements for welfare recipients like the one established by California only goes to show the reasonableness of a law like [this measure]. The National Legislature, where people from Mississippi as well as California are represented, has recognized the need to protect state resources in a time of experimentation and welfare reform. As States like California revamp their total welfare packages, they should have the authority and flexibility to ensure that their new programs are not exploited. Congress has decided that it makes good welfare policy to give the States this power. California has reasonably exercised it through an objective, narrowly tailored residence requirement. I see nothing in the Constitution that should prevent the enforcement of that requirement.

> "Oftentimes it is not the welfare recipients themselves complaining, but others with a vested interest in opposing reform."

Welfare Rights Activists Undermine States' Efforts Toward Welfare Reform

Matthew Berry

At the time the following viewpoint was written (which was before the Supreme Court's decision), Matthew Berry was an attorney with the Washington, D.C.–based Institute for Justice, which filed an amicus curiae (friend of the court) brief in this case. Later Berry was general counsel for the Federal Communications Commission, and in 2010 he ran unsuccessfully for Congress representing the state of Virginia. Here, he argues that although welfare reform is popular with the public, welfare rights activists are attempting to perpetuate the welfare state and sabotage successful reforms. In opposing California's effort to stop people from moving there to collect higher welfare benefits, he says, these activists confuse the genuine right to travel with a nonexistent right to have travel subsidized by the government. The Supreme Court's decision in this case, Berry asserts, will be important not only in itself, but because of the signal it will send to lower courts that are considering other lawsuits brought by welfare advocates.

Matthew Berry, "Assault on Welfare Reform Moves to U.S. Supreme Court," *Intellectual Ammunition*, March/April 1999. Reproduced by permission.

Do welfare recipients have a constitutional right to generous benefits? On January 13, the U.S. Supreme Court took up this issue when it heard oral arguments in *Anderson v. Roe* [the case name was changed to *Saenz v. Roe* when Rita Saenz replaced Eloise Anderson as director of the California Department of Social Services]. In dispute is the constitutionality of California's effort to stop welfare recipients from moving into the Golden State in order to receive higher welfare benefits.

The California statute under attack caps new residents' cash-aid welfare benefits for one year to the level offered by their previous home state. For example, welfare recipients moving from Oklahoma to California would receive an amount equal to Oklahoma's monthly payment—$307 a month—during their first year in California, rather than the $575 a month typically provided by the Golden State.

To most, the California law, explicitly authorized by Congress in the 1996 federal welfare reform legislation, represents a common-sense attempt to protect the state's treasury from new demands for aid. Other states have enacted similar laws in order to stem the inflow of new welfare claimants and thus allow states to concentrate their energies and resources on moving existing recipients from welfare to work.

But to welfare-rights advocates, these laws are an unconstitutional infringement on the right to travel. Confusing the genuine right to migrate from state to state free from government interference with a nonexistent right to have the government subsidize one's travel, opponents of welfare reform have filed several suits seeking to block states from implementing these important initiatives.

Unfortunately, these suits are not an isolated phenomenon. While welfare reform continues to be popular among the general public and politicians of both major parties, organizations committed to the perpetuation of the welfare state, such as the ACLU [American Civil Liberties Union] and National Clearinghouse for Legal Services, have launched a little-noticed but quite dangerous attack on welfare reform in courts across the nation. Their aim is to sabotage virtually every crucial element of current reform efforts—even as the dramatic drop in the number on the nation's welfare rolls demonstrates the success of such policies.

No Right to Welfare Benefits

The U.S. Supreme Court made it clear in the 1970 case of *Dandridge v. Williams* that there is no fundamental right to receive welfare benefits. This has not, however, stopped welfare advocates from deploying a wide range of creative arguments in defense of the failed status quo. In New York City, for instance, students at the City University of New York sued in an attempt to evade the city's requirement that all welfare recipients who are able to work do so in exchange for their benefits. Some 5,000 students claimed they were physically unable to work yet somehow managed to take classes at CUNY [City University of New York].

In Massachusetts, advocates of the status quo are attempting to evade that state's two-year time limit on benefits by claiming that fully one-third of those on the Bay State's welfare rolls are learning disabled and thus cannot work. This assertion no doubt would come as a surprise to the millions of individuals with learning disabilities who are gainfully employed in the United States today.

Oftentimes it is not the welfare recipients themselves complaining, but others with a vested interest in opposing reform. Public employee unions in New York City, for example, have sued in an attempt to prevent workfare participants from performing elementary jobs, such as painting. And in Texas, workers in the state's social services bureaucracy have gone to court in an attempt to block Governor [George W.] Bush's effort to privatize the state's job placement efforts for those on welfare.

Besides insisting that recipients work, another key aim of reformers is to reduce both illegitimacy and teenage pregnancy. A central strategy to accomplishing this goal is to end the practice of increasing a recipient's welfare check each time she has another child. But welfare advocacy organizations have sued to block this change as well. Lawsuits have been filed in both New Jersey and Indiana challenging "family cap" policies, asserting in practical terms that recipients have a constitutional right to a larger handout whenever they have an additional child. Although they lost their federal lawsuit in New Jersey, welfare reform opponents displayed their tenacity by marching right into state court asserting similar claims under the state constitution. Meanwhile, research has revealed that New Jersey's family cap has successfully reduced the birthrate of the Garden State's welfare recipients.

So while *Anderson v. Roe* is important on the merits of the California law itself, it is also critical because the Supreme Court's decision on the case will send a signal to the lower courts presently considering the coordinated flood of lawsuits brought by welfare advocates. Will the Court reaffirm its well-considered refusal to establish a constitutional right to welfare? Or will it open the door to judicial micro-management of each state's social welfare policy? Those heartened by the remarkable success of welfare reform to date should pay close attention to the Court's answer.

"When making the decision to leave an abusive partner, battered women will not be confined by a state's law to limit welfare assistance."

Saenz Will Help Women Who Are Fleeing Abuse

David M. Heger

In the following viewpoint, David M. Heger, a policy analyst for the National Violence Against Women Prevention Research Center at the University of Missouri–St. Louis, points out that the percentage of domestic violence victims is much higher among welfare recipients than among the general population and that some move from state to state to avoid abusive situations. California's law limiting new residents' welfare payments to the amount they would have received in their former state made it almost impossible for them to survive, considering the higher cost of living in California. Although legal scholars will continue to scrutinize the basis of the ruling in Saenz v. Roe *that struck down that law, he says, the Court's decision was a victory for economically disadvantaged women who want to start over in a new state.*

On May 17, 1999, the United States Supreme Court handed down a 7-2 decision striking a provision of the *Personal Responsibility and Work Opportunity Reconciliation Act of 1996* (also known as the *Welfare Reform Bill*) that allowed states to provide lower welfare benefits to new residents. Writing for

David M. Heger, "Saenz Ruling Favors Indigent Women Fleeing Abuse," National Violence Against Women Prevention Research Center, February 5, 2001. Reproduced by permission.

the majority in *Saenz v. Roe*, Justice John Paul Stevens states, "Citizens of the United states, whether rich or poor, have the right to choose to be citizens 'of the State wherein they reside.' The States, however, do not have any right to select their citizens." The State of California argued that the purpose of its 1992 law to limit the amount of welfare assistance available to new residents was not to fence out the indigent, but rather to save the state's taxpayers $10.9 million a year. The Court ruled that this rationale did not justify the state's law. Furthermore, because the law imposed durational residency requirements on a public benefit, the Court decided that it violated the constitutional right to interstate travel or migration.

Many studies have shown that the percentage of welfare recipients who are victims of domestic violence is much higher than the percentage of the general population who suffers violence at home. The rates vary from study to study, but most data indicate that over 50 percent of welfare recipients have experienced abuse at the hands of an intimate partner at least once in their lifetime.

Moving to Escape Abuse

Some victims of domestic violence relocate to a new state of residence to escape the wrath of their abusers. Each of the three original plaintiffs in the case that spurred *Saenz v. Roe* were welfare recipients who had moved to California to flee abusive family circumstances. Under the 1992 California law limiting public assistance, these women were restricted for one year to welfare payments equal to what they had received in their prior states of residence. The amounts they received were several hundred dollars less per month than what California afforded long-term residents on welfare. In fact, what they were afforded during their first year in California was far too little on which to survive, given the state's relatively high cost of living.

The previous federal welfare program, Aid for Families with Dependent Children (AFDC), required the Secretary of the Department of Health and Human Services (HHS) to approve any state alterations on federal law. The Secretary endorsed the new California statute and it was then put into effect. However, based primarily on previous U.S. Supreme Court decisions in *Shapiro v. Thompson* and *Zobel v. Williams*, a federal district court enjoined implementation of [the statute] in *Green v. Anderson*. The Ninth Circuit Court of Appeals affirmed the decision of the lower court. The U.S. Supreme Court agreed to hear the case, but subsequently threw it out after the HHS Secretary's approval of the California law was invalidated in a separate proceeding.

In 1996, Congress reformed the nation's welfare program by replacing AFDC with Temporary Assistance for Needy Families (TANF), which included a provision that validated laws in California and other states to pay lower benefits to newly arrived residents. The district court responded by granting plaintiffs' request for an injunction, declaring the new federal statute to be unconstitutional. The Ninth Circuit affirmed and the case made its way to the nation's highest court.

The Supreme Court affirmed the lower court's ruling in *Saens v. Roe* by relying on the Privileges or Immunities Clause of the Fourteenth Amendment to the Constitution, a provision utilized by the Court so infrequently that many legal scholars had ignored its existence. Chief Justice William Rehnquist opens his dissent with a sardonic assessment of the reasoning of the majority opinion. "The Court today breathes new life into the previously dormant Privileges or Immunities Clause of the Fourteenth Amendment . . ." The clause states that "no state shall make or enforce any law which shall abridge the privileges or immunities of citizens of the United States." In past decisions defending the constitutional right to travel, justices had invoked the Fourteenth Amendment's Equal

Protection Clause, which declares that no state can "deny to any person within its jurisdiction the equal protection of the laws."

Legal scholars will continue to analyze and scrutinize the grounding of the majority opinion in *Saenz*. However, as a practical matter, the ruling is a victory for economically disadvantaged women who want to start new lives in places far away from the source of their abuse. When making the decision to leave an abusive partner, battered women will not be confined by a state's law to limit welfare assistance. As an advocate told the *Washington Post*, "It is a big deal, especially when you consider these folks live on the edge. In some cases, it would mean the difference between paying the rent or not paying it."

> "The Court's effort to distinguish college
> tuition as a portable benefit proves to
> be more illusion than sound principle."

Saenz May Affect Out-of-State College Tuition Laws

Douglas R. Chartier

Douglas R. Chartier is an attorney with the global law firm of Morrison Foerster. Writing while a law student at the University of Michigan, he argues in the following viewpoint that although in the past courts have held that residence requirements for qualifying for in-state college tuition are constitutional, the decision in Saenz v. Roe *may cause that to change. Because* Saenz *shifted the focus in residence-requirement cases from whether they interfere with the right to travel to whether they result in discrimination between old and new residents, in the future such cases should be considered under what courts call "strict scrutiny," which involves special standards for determining the constitutionality of a law. He maintains that under strict scrutiny, treating college students as temporary residents for tuition purposes would clearly be considered unconstitutional.*

After the excitement of getting into the college of her choice wears off, a student may soon wonder how she will pay for her newfound prize. Though higher education is almost always a sound investment given its potentially tremendous return and importance in getting a good job, the cost is daunting—sometimes even prohibitive—for many students. Public

Douglas R. Chartier, "The Toll for Traveling Students: Durational-Residence Requirements for In-State Tuition After *Saenz v. Roe*," *Michigan Law Review*, vol. 104, 2005, pp. 573–75, 577–78, 582–91, 594–98. Copyright © 2005 by The Michigan Law Review Association. Reproduced by permission of the publisher and author.

undergraduate and graduate schools are an attractive option for many students because of lower tuitions. Yet state universities deny many students the full measure of this benefit.

Public universities usually charge significantly higher tuition rates to out-of-state students than in-state students. A nonresident student may find herself paying as much as three times what her resident counterparts pay. Consequently, a student's classification as a resident or nonresident may determine whether she can afford higher education. State statutes and school regulations often require that students have resided in the state for at least a year before they can be classified as residents for tuition purposes. As a result, state colleges frequently deny many students the benefit of lower tuition for at least a year, regardless of their intentions to make the state their permanent home.

These sorts of waiting periods, which require that a person have resided in a state for a particular period of time before she is entitled to a benefit, are called durational-residence requirements. Durational-residence requirements raise a red flag for many constitutional law scholars because the Supreme Court has struck down many—though not all—of them. It is therefore unsurprising that many lawyers and scholars have argued that durational-residence requirements for in-state tuition are unconstitutional. Nevertheless, no court has found these requirements unconstitutional.

Residence Requirements and the Right to Travel

The Supreme Court has repeatedly recognized that durational-residence requirements implicate the fundamental right to travel. In *Shapiro v. Thompson*, the Court struck down one-year durational-residence requirements for welfare benefits in Connecticut, Pennsylvania, and Washington, D.C. . . .

Perhaps recognizing the myriad durational-residence requirements in existence, the Court carefully qualified its holding. In what would haunt future judicial review of durational-residence requirements for in-state tuition, the Court stated in an infamous footnote that its holding implied "no view of the validity of waiting-period *or* residence requirements determining eligibility to vote, *eligibility for tuition-free education,* to obtain a license to practice a profession, to hunt or fish, and so forth" [emphasis added]. . . .

In its most recent review of a durational-residence requirement in *Saenz v. Roe,* the Supreme Court threw many new surprises into the constitutional analysis of these laws. At issue was a California law that limited new residents, for the first year of their residence in the state, to the welfare benefits they would have received in their prior states of residence. . . . In its defense, California claimed that the law would save the state $10.9 million per year in welfare costs. California also argued that the law had no punitive effect because newly arrived welfare recipients received the same welfare benefits they would have in their previous states of residence; the law thus made them no worse off. The state was likely trying to avoid *Shapiro*'s call for strict scrutiny when a law "penalizes" the exercise of the right to travel.

An unconvinced Court struck down the law. . . . The Court held that the law failed strict scrutiny because the state's justification of saving money had no relevance to the duration of the recipients' residence in California or their prior states of residence.

Saenz's critical innovation was to broaden the analysis from *Shapiro*'s severe-penalties rule. . . . The Court rejected California's justification that the requirement only "incidentally" affected the right to travel. The Court then concluded that because a newly arrived citizen has a right to be treated equally in her state, a discriminatory classification itself serves as a penalty. Thus, the Court shifted the focus from severe penalties upon the exercise of the right to travel to discrimination against those who have exercised that right.

Like the footnote in *Shapiro, Saenz* included language that would persuade other courts to limit its future applicability. The Court asserted that the welfare benefits in question could only be consumed while the recipient remained in California. The Court then established a "portability distinction" between welfare benefits and "readily portable benefit[s], such as divorce or a *college education*, that will be enjoyed after [citizens of other states] return to their original domicile." [emphasis added] This language would later serve to thwart efforts in lower courts to strike down durational-residence requirements for in-state tuition.

Both before and after the *Saenz* decision, challenges to durational-residence requirements for in-state tuition at public colleges and universities were invariably unsuccessful. The Supreme Court has never conducted a significant analysis of this issue. The Court has held that states may restrict tuition-free education to bona fide residents. Therefore, a fortiori [by even stronger reasoning], the Constitution allows states to charge nonresidents higher tuition than bona fide residents. . . .

An Unprincipled Distinction

Upon close inspection, the Court's effort to distinguish college tuition as a portable benefit proves to be more illusion than sound principle. The notion that college tuition is portable is predicated on the idea that one could receive the benefit of education and still reap benefits from it after moving to another state. Consequently, the Court feared that eliminating durational-residence requirements for this class of benefits would encourage people to move to states only as long as necessary to obtain the desired benefit. To a great extent, however, welfare payments provide just as portable a benefit as college education. . . .

Portability cannot distinguish welfare from tuition subsidies. Under a temporally limited view of welfare benefits—which in *Saenz* were cash payments—the benefit appears nonportable in the sense that the recipient will usually immediately spend the money and be unable to take it out of the state. This view, however, fails to recognize the ultimate utility of welfare. Critically, welfare is a portable investment in human capital, like a tuition subsidy; further, both can be similarly portable. As Chief Justice [William] Rehnquist pointed out in his dissent to *Saenz*, the point of welfare is to give an indigent person much needed cash so that she can receive training, education, and time to look for a job. Consequently, though the cash payment is consumed immediately in-state, the fruits of the benefit remain with the recipient and may benefit her wherever she goes. Similarly, reduced in-state tuition is something that a student consumes while in-state, but the benefit of access to a college education will benefit her anywhere. . . .

In trying to prevent benefit seekers from harming the states to which they flock, the Court fashioned a portability distinction that nonetheless was irrelevant to that harm. The Court specifically viewed this harm as encompassing people coming to a state only to avail themselves of attractive "portable" benefits, then leaving shortly thereafter because they could reap the rewards of the benefits elsewhere. States would be inundated by benefit seekers who would soon leave the state after obtaining the costly benefits that brought them in the first place, thus depriving the state of contributions from the recipient before and after the conferral.

Critically, portability is of little importance even when one considers the potential harm from the influx of welfare hunters. Even assuming that portability constitutes a workable distinction, this distinction is irrelevant; whether a benefit is portable may not change a new resident's incentive to leave a state shortly after arriving. This seemed to be the case with the welfare benefits in question in *Saenz*. California residents could receive welfare benefits for no longer than five years. A person who came to California only to obtain its more generous welfare benefits would have no incentive to remain after the state has cut her off from those benefits. Those who have the means to leave—certainly a possibility considering that they had the ability to come to the state in the first place—can leave. Moreover, if the recipient were able to reach self-sufficiency at or before the end of the welfare period, she could leave the state before making any significant contributions to the local economy. Even worse, those who have neither reached self-sufficiency nor have the ability to leave present another problem: they will remain in the state without contributing to the economy, but may still avail themselves of other valuable state benefits.

Students may present less potential harm to states than welfare recipients. A similar flight risk is present with in-state tuition seekers: there is a risk that an out-of-state student will remain in the state only for the four years in which she obtains her undergraduate education. Concededly, it is more plausible that students have the ability to leave the state. Unlike welfare recipients, however, it is less likely that the state will have to deal with people who must remain even after availing themselves of the state benefits but cannot contribute to the state economy. Consequently, portability has little connection to the harm to states in the case of both welfare and tuition. . . .

Discrimination of Old and New Residents

Much case law declining to apply strict scrutiny to durational-residence requirements for in-state tuition did so because the courts did not think that the waiting periods chilled or deterred migration into the state. That could certainly be the case; in many states, a newly arrived student knows that she will be entitled to reduced tuition after her first year of education, at least if she can establish her intent to remain in the state permanently.

In adopting its nondiscrimination rule, *Saenz* expressly rejected that deterrence or chilling of migration was necessary for strict scrutiny to apply. The Court stated that it was not concerned solely with actual deterrence to interstate migration. . . .

In light of *Saenz*, the degree to which a new resident is penalized is no longer critical. The *Shapiro* severe-penalties rule, by definition, requires asking whether the denial or in-state tuition operates as a penalty upon the exercise of the right to travel. Arguably, the penalty upon a student is not very significant because she is not completely foreclosed from obtaining higher education in her new state of residence; she could still attend a public university in that state, though at a higher tuition rate for a set period of time. Moreover, out-of-state tuition for *some* students may not be much worse than their other realistic options. . . .

Saenz renders this inquiry irrelevant. The Court rejected California's defense that the welfare recipients were no worse off than they were in their previous states because their welfare benefits would be the same. . . . Because the focus is now on whether there is discrimination between new and old residents, it seems that a state's denial of in-state tuition to those who have resided in the state for less than a requisite period of time is sufficient discrimination to infringe upon the right to travel. The concept of penalty thus drops out of the picture; disparate treatment is the triggering condition. . . .

Worthy of Strict Scrutiny

Courts have long held that they will sometimes review durational-residence requirements under strict scrutiny even when the denied benefit or right is not essential to one's survival. For example, the Supreme Court held in [*Dunn v.*] *Blumstein* that durational-residence requirements implicating important rights such as the right to vote must satisfy strict scrutiny. . . .

Of course, because these decisions involve voting and elections, they do not necessarily imply that the right covers college tuition. A durational-residence requirement for voting involves a fundamental right, whereas a durational-residence requirement for in-state tuition involves a benefit to which one has no fundamental right. . . .

Nevertheless, other decisions by the Supreme Court show that the right to travel extends to important benefits that are neither fundamental rights nor important to maintaining democracy. . . .

Education is an especially important state service. Concededly, the Supreme Court has held that there is no fundamental right to education. Furthermore, lower courts have consistently refused to equate education with the basic necessities of life. Courts have, however, recognized that education is a very important benefit. Consequently, education is, at the very least, distinguishable from other types of benefits whose denial may seem more trivial, like obtaining a license to hunt or fish. . . .

A principal contention against use of strict scrutiny for in-state tuition could be the Supreme Court's summary affirmations of *Starns* [*v. Malkerson*] and *Sturgis* [*v. Washington*]. . . . Those district courts upheld durational-residence requirements for in-state tuition under rational basis review. In deciding *Saenz*, the Court never disapproved or overruled these cases. In fact, the Court may have implicitly reaffirmed them through its fashioning of the portability distinction, which it supported by citation to *Vlandis* [*v. Kline*]'s dicta [nonprecedent-setting statements by a judge] concerning waiting periods for in-state tuition.

Nonetheless, *Starns* and *Sturgis* cannot stand as principled decisions in light of the reasoning behind *Saenz*. The Court issued no opinion in either case, leaving only the district court opinions as windows to its thought processes. The district courts distinguished *Shapiro* and its call for strict scrutiny on the grounds that (1) they did not think that the requirements were created with the purpose or effect of deterring out-of-state students from attending in-state universities, and (2) the requirements did not deny the students the basic necessities of life. . . .

These lower court decisions are no longer valid. The reasoning of these opinions, which relies upon *Shapiro's* severe-penalties rule, is plainly inconsistent with the nondiscrimination rule established by *Saenz.* Moreover, the portability distinction is a fiction that cannot shield in-state tuition from *Saenz's* new rule.

Strict Scrutiny of Residence Requirements

When one reviews in-state tuition durational-residence requirements under strict scrutiny, their unconstitutionality is quickly revealed. In order to survive strict scrutiny, the requirement must be narrowly tailored to advance a compelling state interest. States commonly claim that these requirements are necessary to achieve partial cost equalization between new and old residents, facilitate residency determinations, and limit reduced tuition to those likely to make future contributions to the state's economy. The justifications that have been or are likely to be advanced for these requirements either are not compelling or use means not narrowly tailored to achieve them.

The justification that the requirement is necessary to achieve partial cost equalization is not compelling. The basis of this justification is that states may collect lower tuition from those who have made recent contributions to the state or have recently spent money in the state for a brief period before enrolling in a state school. Thus, until a new resident makes some contribution to the state's welfare, she is not entitled to the same privileges as longer term residents. A very similar justification failed scrutiny in *Shapiro. Shapiro* rejected distinctions between new and old residents based upon contributions they had made to the community in the form of taxes. The Court held the contribution justification constitutionally impermissible despite the state's valid interest in maintaining its fiscal integrity. Under a contrary ruling, states would be able to apportion or deny benefits such as schools, parks, or police and fire protection based upon a citizen's past tax contributions. The same constitutional objection applies to contributions made directly to the state economy since both involve benefits conferred to the local community. . . .

These durational-residence requirements cannot be constitutionally permissible on the ground that they are the only way to determine residency and thus as narrowly tailored as practically feasible. These requirements are not the only method of determining a person's residency status. Some colleges look to other indicators, avoiding a strict durational-residence requirement. Similarly, in determining one's residency for tax purposes, California lists thirteen factors—none of which involve the length of stay in the state—to determine residency and calls for comparing these factors across the different states to which a person has ties. Many of these, such as location of social ties, family, and principal residence, apply to students. . . .

The justification that in-state tuition should be limited to those willing to make future contributions to the state economy should fail because a durational-residence requirement is not narrowly tailored to that end. This justification only makes sense when the waiting period is applied to non-bona-fide residents; a bona fide resident would intend to remain in the state and make the desired future contributions. The requirement would thus lack even a rational basis if a state intentionally applied it to all new residents, bona fide or otherwise. . . .

Finally, even if *Saenz* can be read to establish a compelling state interest in restricting the apportionment of portable benefits, a durational-residence requirement would not be narrowly tailored to achieve that end. The concern surrounding the portability of a benefit is that a temporary resident will leave after acquiring the benefit and enjoy it after returning to her previous state of residence. The waiting period, however, would be both overinclusive and underinclusive. It would burden new bona fide residents who genuinely wish to take advantage of the benefit in their new state of residence; it would also fail to account for residents who have no intention of remaining in the state but have lived in the state for just a little longer than the requisite waiting period. Such a blunt tool cannot pass the rigors of strict scrutiny.

Implications of *Saenz v. Roe* for Students

Saenz thus has implications far beyond what the Supreme Court likely envisioned. The Court's attempt to cabin the decision through the portability distinction cannot serve as a principled reason to limit the scope of its holding. *Saenz*'s nondiscrimination rule flows over at least the broad range of state benefits that other case law has held significant enough to be protected by the fundamental right to travel. The similarity of in-state tuition to these other benefits, combined with the nondiscrimination rule, leads logically toward strict scrutiny review of these waiting periods. Much to the delight of traveling students, the states are unlikely to offer any justification that will pass constitutional muster under that standard. *Saenz*'s broad impact can certainly spell trouble for other durational-residence requirements that have yet to be declared unconstitutional. The decision truly ensures that once one decides to make a state her indefinite home, she may not be treated as a temporary interloper. States must account for this constitutional protection in fashioning their residency requirements.

Organizations to Contact

The editors have compiled the following list of organizations concerned with the issues debated in this book. The descriptions are derived from materials provided by the organizations. All have publications or information available for interested readers. The list was compiled on the date of publication of the present volume; the information provided here may change. Be aware that many organizations take several weeks or longer to respond to inquiries, so allow as much time as possible.

Administration for Children and Families (ACF)
Office of Family Assistance, Washington, DC 20447
(202) 401-9275 • fax: (202) 205-5887
Web site: www.acf.hhs.gov

The Administration for Children and Families is a branch of the U.S. Department of Health and Human Services, the United States government's principal agency for protecting the health of all Americans and providing essential human services, especially for those who are least able to help themselves. It operates the Temporary Assistance for Needy Families (TANF) program, which replaced the former federal welfare program in 1997. The fact sheet about TANF explains what it is and the qualifications for receiving aid.

American Enterprise Institute (AEI)
1150 Seventeenth St. NW, Ste. 1100, Washington, DC 20036
(202) 862-5800 • fax: (202) 862-7177
Web site: www.aei.org

The American Enterprise Institute (AEI) for Public Policy Research is a private, nonpartisan, not-for-profit institution dedicated to research and education on issues of government, politics, economics, and social welfare. Advocating for limited government and competitive private enterprise, it conducts research in economic policy studies, social and political studies, and defense and foreign policy studies, and supports the Welfare Reform Academy at the University of Maryland School of Public Policy. Publications available on its Web site include the articles "Social Welfare Conservatism" and "Attitudes About Welfare Reform," as well as abstracts of AEI Press books, including *The Poverty of "The Poverty Rate."*

Cato Institute

1000 Massachusetts Ave. NW, Washington, DC   20001-5403
(202) 842-0200 • fax: (202) 842-3490
Web site: www.cato.org

Founded in 1977, the Cato Institute is a nonprofit public policy research foundation that encourages limited government, individual liberty, free markets, and peace and strives to achieve greater involvement of the intelligent, concerned lay public in questions of policy and the proper role of government. Its research divisions include Education and Child Policy; Health, Welfare, and Entitlements; Tax and Budget Policy; and others. Extensive online library includes reviews, journals, articles, opinion columns, videos, and policy studies, and a dedicated section for students includes blogs and an "Ask the Expert" feature.

Center on Budget and Policy Priorities (CBPP)

820 First St. NE, Ste. 510, Washington, DC   20002
(202) 408-1080 • fax: (202) 408-1056
e-mail: center@cbpp.org
Web site: www.cbpp.org

The Center on Budget and Policy Priorities conducts research and analysis to help shape public debates over proposed budget and tax policies and to help ensure that policy makers consider the needs of low-income families and individuals in these debates. It also develops policy options to alleviate poverty. Its Web site contains a section with extensive information about Temporary Assistance for Needy Families, the current government welfare program.

Center on Law and Social Policy (CLASP)
1200 Eighteenth St. NW, Ste. 200, Washington, DC   20036
(202) 906-8000 • fax: (202) 842-2885
Web site: www.clasp.org

Center on Law and Social Policy's mission is to develop and advocate for policies at the federal, state, and local levels that improve the lives of low-income people. In particular, it seeks policies that work to strengthen families and create pathways to education and work. Its Web site contains news and detailed information about welfare and other government programs on a state-by-state basis.

Coalition on Human Needs (CHN)
1120 Connecticut Ave. NW, Ste. 312, Washington, DC   20036
(202) 223-2532 • fax: (202) 223-2538
Web site: www.chn.org

The Coalition on Human Needs is an alliance of national organizations working together to promote public policies that address the needs of low-income and other vulnerable populations. Its Web site contains news and policy analyses concerning many programs that provide aid to the needy, plus links to all its member organizations.

The Heritage Foundation
214 Massachusetts Ave. NE, Washington, DC   20002
(202) 546-4400 • fax: (202) 546.8328
e-mail: info@heritage.org
Web site: www.heritage.org

Founded in 1973, the Heritage Foundation is a research and educational institute whose mission is to formulate and promote conservative public policies based on the principles of free enterprise, limited government, individual freedom, traditional American values, and a strong national defense. The foundations works with a wide range of domestic and foreign issues, including the economy, education, and welfare. Its Web site collects press releases, policy reports, and opinion columns, with titles including "Memo to Congress: Make Jobs, Not Work" and "Welfare Reform Turns Ten: Evidence Shows Reduced Dependence, Poverty," and offers a blog, The Foundry.

National Center for Children in Poverty (NCCP)
215 W. 125th St., 3rd Fl., New York, NY 10027
(646) 284-9600 • fax: (646) 284-9623
e-mail: info@nccp.org
Web site: www.nccp.org

The National Center for Children in Poverty, a nonprofit division of the Mailman School of Public Health at Columbia University, is the nation's leading public policy center dedicated to promoting the economic security, health, and well-being of America's low-income families and children. It uses research to inform policy and practice with the goal of ensuring positive outcomes for the next generation. Its Web site contains many detailed articles and reports on various topics related to poverty.

National Center for Law and Economic Justice (NCLEJ)
275 Seventh Ave., Ste. 1506, New York, NY 10001-6708
(212) 633-6967
e-mail: info@nclej.org
Web site: www.nclej.org

The mission of the National Center for Law and Economic Justice is to advance the cause of economic justice for low-income families, individuals, and communities across the country. It is a national leader in using litigation to make sure that low-income people get the benefits they are entitled to and that government agencies administer programs fairly. Its Web site contains information about its many activities and back issues of its newsletter.

Urban Institute
2100 M St. NW, Washington, DC 20037
(202) 833-7200

Web site: www.urban.org

The Urban Institute is a nonpartisan organization that gathers data, conducts research, evaluates programs, offers technical assistance overseas, and educates Americans on social and economic issues in order to foster sound public policy and effective government. Its Web site contains many articles on welfare/poverty programs, in addition to other topics.

For Further Research

Books

Mimi Abramovitz, *Regulating the Lives of Women: Social Welfare Policy from Colonial Times to the Present*. Boston: South End Press, 1999.

Randy Albelda and Ann Withorn, eds., *Lost Ground: Welfare Reform, Poverty, and Beyond*. Boston: South End Press, 2002.

Mary Jo Bane and David R. Ellwood, *Welfare Realities: From Rhetoric to Reform*. Cambridge, MA: Harvard University Press, 1994.

Edgar K. Browning, *Stealing from Each Other: How the Welfare State Robs Americans of Money and Spirit*. Westport, CT: Praeger, 2008.

Elizabeth Bussiere, *(Dis)entitling the Poor: Constitutional Welfare Rights in the Supreme Court, 1965–1975*. University Park: Pennsylvania State University Press, 1997.

Martha F. Davis, *Brutal Need: Lawyers and the Welfare Rights Movement, 1960–1973*. New Haven, CT: Yale University Press, 1993.

Joe R. Feagin, *Subordinating the Poor: Welfare and American Beliefs*. Englewood Cliffs, NJ: Prentice-Hall, 1975.

Martin Gilens, *Why Americans Hate Welfare: Race, Media, and the Politics of Antipoverty Policy*. Chicago: University of Chicago Press, 2000.

John Gilliom, *Overseers of the Poor: Surveillance, Resistance, and the Limits of Privacy*. Chicago: University of Chicago Press, 2001.

Gertrude Schaffner Goldberg, *Washington's New Poor Law: Welfare Reform and the Roads Not Taken, 1935 to the Present*. New York: Apex Press, 2001.

Joel F. Handler and Yeheskel Hasenfeld, *Blame Welfare, Ignore Poverty and Inequality*. New York: Cambridge University Press, 2007.

Ron Haskins, *Work over Welfare: The Inside Story of the 1996 Welfare Reform Law*. Washington, DC: Brookings Institution Press, 2006.

Sharon Hays, *Flat Broke with Children: Women in the Age of Welfare Reform*. New York: Oxford University Press, 2003.

Michael B. Katz, *In the Shadow of the Poorhouse: A Social History of Welfare in America*. New York: BasicBooks, 1996.

Daniel C. Kramer, *The Price of Rights: The Courts, Government Largesse, and Fundamental Liberties*. New York: Peter Lang, 2004.

Lawrence M. Mead, *Beyond Entitlement: The Social Obligations of Citizenship*. New York: Free Press, 1986.

R. Shep Melnick, *Between the Lines: Interpreting Welfare Rights*. Washington, DC: Brookings Institution Press, 1994.

Suzanne Mettler, *Dividing Citizens: Gender and Federalism in New Deal Public Policy*. Ithaca, NY: Cornell University Press, 1998.

Jennifer Mittelstadt, *From Welfare to Workfare: The Unintended Consequences of Liberal Reform, 1945–1965*. Chapel Hill: University of North Carolina Press, 2005.

Charles Murray, *Losing Ground: American Social Policy, 1950–1980*. New York: BasicBooks, 1994.

E. Joshua Rosenkranz and Bernard Schwartz, eds., *Reason and Passion: Justice Brennan's Enduring Influence*. New York: Norton, 1997.

Anna Marie Smith, *Welfare Reform and Sexual Regulation*. New York: Cambridge University Press, 2007.

Periodicals

Akhil Reed Amar, "Lost Clause," *New Republic*, June 14, 1999.

Joan Biskupic, "New-Resident Limits on Welfare Rejected; Court Stresses Equality," *Washington Post*, May 18, 1999.

Laura Butterbaugh, "Disparate Welfare Benefits Ruled Illegal," *Off Our Backs*, June 1999.

William Chapman, "Man-in-House Rule in Child Aid Voided," *Washington Post*, June 18, 1968.

Martha F. Davis, "The Evolving Right to Travel: *Saenz v. Roe*," *Publius*, Spring 1999.

Martha F. Davis, Risa E. Kaufman, and Henry A. Freedman, "The Road Now Taken: The Privileges or Immunities Clause and the Right to Travel," *Clearinghouse Review*, November/December 1999.

Fred P. Graham, "High Court Upsets City Rule on Cutoff in Welfare," *New York Times*, March 24, 1970.

Linda Greenhouse, "Citizenship Has Its Privileges; The Court Resurrects a Civil War-Era Ideal," *New York Times*, May 23, 1999.

———, "New Look at an 'Obscure' Ruling, Twenty Years Later," *New York Times*, May 11, 1990.

———, "The Supreme Court: Citizens' Rights; Newcomers to States Have Right to Equal Welfare, Justices Rule," *New York Times*, May 18, 1999.

————, "Supreme Court Hears Welfare Case," *New York Times*, January 14, 1999.

Jane Gross, "Poor Seekers of Good Life Flock to California, as Middle Class Moves Away; Sun, Safety and State Aid Lure One Family," *New York Times*, December 29, 1991.

Carol Honsa, "Mothers Welcome Welfare Decision," *Washington Post*, June 19, 1968.

Adam Liptak, "Full Constitutional Protection for Some, but No Privacy for the Poor," *New York Times*, July 16, 2007.

New York Times, "Judge Blocks California Cuts in Welfare to New Residents," January 30, 1993.

————, "The Supreme Court: Excerpts from Court's Welfare Ruling and Rehnquist's Dissent," May 18, 1999.

Alain L. Sanders, "Supreme Court Nixes 'Two Class' Welfare," *Time*, May 17, 1999.

Debra J. Saunders, "A Workable Plan to Cut Welfare Spending," *Wall Street Journal*, western ed., March 27, 1991.

Israel Shenker, "New Breed of Lawyer Serving Poor," *New York Times*, August 30, 1969.

Danielle Starkey, "Pete to Immigrants: 'Don't Huddle Here.' Governor Says Breathing Here Ain't Free," *California Journal*, March 1992.

Time, "The National Welfare: Trying to End the Nightmare," February 8, 1971.

————, "Welfare: Revolt of the Nonpersons," July 21, 1967.

Internet Sources

Randy Albelda and Heather Boushey, "From Welfare to Poverty," Institute for America's Future, August 23, 2006. www.tompaine.com.

Peter Edelman, "Welfare and the Poorest of the Poor," *Dissent*, Fall 2009. www.dissentmagazine.org.

Bill Frezza, "Making Sure the Poor Are Always with Us," *Real Clear Markets*, April 13, 2009. www.realclear markets.com.

William H. Mellor, "A Right to Welfare?" *Reason*, October 1994. http://reason.com.

Cathy Young, "The Problem of Poverty: Why the Left and Right Have Little Serious to Say," *Reason*, May 18, 2005. http://reason.com.

Index